The Free Methodist Church:
A Bibliography

by

Francine E. Walls

First Fruits Press
Wilmore, Kentucky
c2016

The Free Methodist Church: A Bibliography. By Francine E. Walls

First Fruits Press, ©2016

Previously published by the Free Methodist Historical Center, ©1977.

ISBN: 9781621714644 (print) 9781621714767 (digital) 9781621715115 (kindle)

Digital version at http:http://place.asburyseminary.edu/freemethodistbooks/7/

Walls, Francine E.

    The free methodist church: a bibliography / by Francine E. Walls

    ii, 102 pages; 21 cm.

    Wilmore, Kentucky : First Fruits Press, ©2016.

Reprint. Previously published: Winona Lake, Indiana : Free Methodist Historical Center, ©1977.
ISBN: 9781621714767 (pbk.)

    1. Free Methodist Church of North America -- Bibliography. I. Title.

BX8417.W34 2016

Cover design by Jonathan Ramsay

asburyseminary.edu
800.2ASBURY
204 North Lexington Avenue
Wilmore, Kentucky 40390

First Fruits
THE ACADEMIC OPEN PRESS OF ASBURY SEMINARY

First Fruits Press
The Academic Open Press of Asbury Theological Seminary
204 N. Lexington Ave., Wilmore, KY 40390
859-858-2236
first.fruits@asburyseminary.edu
asbury.to/firstfruits

THE FREE METHODIST CHURCH:

A Bibliography

by Francine E. Walls

Free Methodist Historical Center
Free Methodist Headquarters
Winona Lake, Indiana 46590
1977

Price

1 copy $3.00
2 copies $5.00
Includes postage & handling.
Please send payment with order.
Order from Free Methodist Historical Center.

Printed in U.S.A.
by
Free Methodist Publishing House
Winona Lake, Indiana 46590

PREFACE

The purpose of compiling a bibliography on Free Methodism
is to identify a body of works that interpret the lives,
beliefs, traditions, and labor of those within the denomination. This bibliography is a partially annotated union
list with location symbols for most cited works housed at
the Free Methodist Historical Center, Seattle Pacific University, Roberts Wesleyan College and Spring Arbor College.
Works such as encyclopedias do not have location symbols
as they are widely available at public and academic libra-
ries.

The authors are primarily Free Methodist except for those
in general categories such as History Handbooks whose
works are included because of their references to Free
Methodism. The works cited in categories with exclusively
Free Methodist authors such as Doctrinal Works are compre-
hensive while works in the general areas represent a selected portion of material available. Only a small number
of unpublished manuscripts from the Free Methodist Historical Center and Roberts Wesleyan College are included.
These, perhaps, require a separate publication. Works
published by missionaries for use on the mission field are
for the most part excluded.

Primary and secondary works are not differentiated. Ar-
rangement of all works is by subject.

I wish to express my appreciation for assistance in pro-
viding needed information to Ms. Marilyn Starr, Spring
Arbor College; Dr. Cathy Stonehouse, Mrs. Debra Chisholm
and Mrs. Marion Groesbeck of the Free Methodist World
Headquarters, and Mrs. Louise Campbell of Roberts Wesleyan
College. Mrs. Evelyn Mottweiler of the Free Methodist
Historical Center provided me with extensive information
on the Historical Center collection and with her thorough
knowledge of Free Methodist History and organization acted
as a sounding board for my ideas. She and her father,
Bishop L. R. Marston assisted with unfailing patience. I
wish to thank them especially.

Francine E. Walls
Seattle Pacific University

This work is lovingly dedicated to
Kenneth and Christian.

TABLE OF CONTENTS

ABBREVIATIONS

Locations:

FMHC   Free Methodist Historical Center
RWC   Roberts Wesleyan College
SAC   Spring Arbor College
SPU   Seattle Pacific University

n.d.   no publishing date given or located
n.p.   no publisher given or located
?   date of publication unverified or unknown

APOLOGETICS

ROBERTS, Benjamin Titus. Why Another Sect? Containing a
   Review of Articles by Bishop Simpson and others on the
   Free Methodist Church. Rochester, New York, 1879.
   FMHC   RWC   SAC   SPU

"The author seeks to clarify the issues of 1860 that forced
the organization of the Free Methodist Church, in view of
the claims by some within the Methodist Episcopal Church
who allegedly had distorted the facts concerning a so-
called "Nazarite" organization and other matters."
L. R. Marston.

BIBLIOGRAPHY

BUNDY, David D. Keswick: A Bibliographic Introduction to
    the Higher Life Movement. Occasional Bibliographic Pa-
    per of the B. L. Fisher Library Series, No. 3. Wilmore,
    Kentucky: B. L. Fisher Library, Asbury Theological Sem-
    inary, 1975. FMHC   SPU

Reference to Free Methodism, p. 45.

DAYTON, Donald M. The American Holiness Movement: A Bib-
    liographic Introduction. Occasional Bibliographic Paper
    of the B. L. Fisher Library Series, No. 1. Wilmore,
    Kentucky: B. L. Fisher Library, Asbury Theological Sem-
    inary, 1971. FMHC   SPU

Scattered references to Free Methodism. Bibliographic es-
say on works in history, biography, periodicals, missions,
preaching, etc. within the Holiness Movement.

JONES, Charles Edwin. A Guide to the Study of the Holiness
    Movement. Metuchen, New Jersey: Scarecrow Press and
    American Theological Library Association, 1974.
    FMHC   SAC   SPU   RWC

FM - pp. 306-325. Citations are arranged by denomination
within the Holiness Movement and then by subject. Excellent resource.

METHODIST Union Catalog: Pre-1976 Imprints. Kenneth E.
    Rowe, ed. Metuchen, New Jersey: The Scarecrow Press,
    1975. FMHC   SPU

For researchers in Methodist history, this contains annotated citations in author sequence.

NAZARENE Theological Seminary. Master Bibliography of
    Holiness Works. Kansas City, Missouri: Beacon Hill
    Press, 1965. 45pp. RWC   FMHC

BIOGRAPHY AND AUTOBIOGRAPHY

See also Mission Fields - Biography and History

ALLAN, David. From the Lumber Camp to the Ministry. The Autobiography of Rev. David Allan. Toronto, Ontario: Evangelical Publishers, 1938. FMHC

Rev. Allan served the Free Methodist Church many years in West Ontario Conference. History of this conference is included.

ANDERSON, Dorothy E. Man of Compassion: Carl Eric Anderson. Glimpses of "Mr. Great-heart" in Action. Essex Junction, Vermont: By author, 1966. FMHC RWC

Carl Anderson was a Free Methodist General Conference evangelist for a time and later pioneered Free Methodist work in Ireland.

ANDREWS, Edwin Alvia. Reminiscent Musings. Spring Arbor, Michigan: By author, 1926. 113pp. FMHC SPU RWC

"Edwin Andrews led a splinter movement organized as the Full Gospel Union which failed to prosper. The author was a man of ability, but as this quaint book reflects, was unduly subjective." L. R. Marston

ARCHER, A. C. The Man with a Thorn in his Flesh. Winona Lake, Indiana: Light and Life Press, 1930. FMHC RWC

A. C. Archer was one of Free Methodism's most successful evangelists notwithstanding the "thorn," a speech defect. Autobiography.

BACKENSTOE, Martin John. Triumphant Living: A Stewardship Report. Kutztown, Pennsylvania: Kutztown Publishing Co., 1949. FMHC RWC

Information on the history of Chili Seminary is also included. Autobiography.

BAKER, H. E. Sackcloth and Purple. Indianapolis, Indiana:
   Pilgrim Publishing House, 1945.   FMHC

H. E. Baker was an evangelist in the Pittsburgh Conference.
Autobiography.

BEERS, Adelaide Lionne. The Romance of a Consecrated Life:
   A Biography of Alexander Beers. Chicago, Illinois:
   Free Methodist Publishing House, 1922. 351pp.
   FMHC   RWC   SPU

BLACK, Harry. From Newsboy to Preacher: The Story of My
   Life. By author, 193?. 172pp. FMHC   RWC

Harry Black was a widely travelled Free Methodist Evangelist.

BLEWS, Richard R. Master Workmen: Biographies of the
   Deceased Bishops of the Free Methodist Church. Light
   and Life Press, 1939, 393pp.   FMHC   RWC   SAC

X BLEWS, Richard R. Master Workmen: Biographies of the
   Late Bishops of the Free Methodist Church During Her
   First Century, 1860-1960. Centennial Edition. Winona
   Lake, Indiana: Light and Life Press, 1960. 303pp.
   FMHC   RWC   SPU

BOSCO, Mrs. N. A. Rye Field to Pulpit: The Life Story of
   Rev. N. A. Bosko. Picton, Ontario, Canada: Picton
   Gazette Publishing Co., 1968.   FMHC

CARPENTER, Adella P. Ellen Lois Roberts: Life and Writings. Chicago, Illinois: Free Methodist Publishing
   House, 1926. FMHC   RWC   SPU

Diaries and letters by the wife of Benjamin Titus Roberts,
the principal founder of Free Methodism. She wrote of
life in connection with her husband and his work.

CAVNAUGH, John. Travels, Trials, Sights and Scenes of
    John Cavnaugh, pastor in the New York Conference, Free
    Methodist Church. n.p., 1896. FMHC

CHAPMAN, Mary Weems. Mother Cobb or Sixty Years' Walk
    with God. Chicago, Illinois: T. B. Arnold, 1896.
    FMHC

Mother Cobb of Northern Illinois remained a Methodist
Episcopal but was a friend of Free Methodism. She men-
tions the Free Methodist Church often in the journals recorded in this book.

COOKE, Sarah A. The Handmaiden of the Lord, or Wayside
    Sketches. Chicago, Illinois: T. B. Arnold, 1896.
    406pp. FMHC RWC

"Two Free Methodist women exhorted and prayed with D. L.
Moody after which his ministry was greatly blessed. Sarah
Cooke was one of them. She was a member of the Free Meth-
odist Church and an outstanding contributor to early Free
Methodism in Chicago and the Mid-west." - Evelyn Mott-
weiler. Autobiography.

DAMON, C. M. Sketches and Incidents: or Reminiscences of
    Interest in the Life of the Author with an Appendix
    containing treatises on "The Ministrations of the
    Spirit," "National Religion," and "On Holiness," with
    other matter. Chicago, Illinois: Free Methodist Pub-
    lishing House, 1900. 355pp. FMHC SAC

DAMON, C. M. Sketches and Incidents: or Reminiscenses of
    Interest in the Life of the Author.... Chicago, Illi-
    nois: Free Methodist Publishing House, 1908. 366pp.
    RWC

DAVIS, La Verne Ball. Daddy is a Layman: A True Tale of
    Laughs, Loves and Ladders. Los Angeles, California:
    Cowman Publishing, 1953. FMHC RWC

Biography of Arthur G. Ball, Free Methodist businessman.

DAWSON, Franklin Raymond. Life Sketch and Sermons of Rev. B. C. Dewey. Chicago, Illinois: Free Methodist Publishing House, 1929. 102pp. FMHC SPU

Washington State Free Methodist minister.

DAWSON, Louise S. Vital Faith. Seattle, Washington: By author, 1962. FMHC RWC

Franklin Raymond Dawson was an outstanding minister of the Free Methodist Pacific Northwest Conference in Washington State. Biography written by his wife.

DeVOIST, Myron. Footprints in My Life or The Story Told In Rhyme. n.p., 1920. FMHC

Rev. DeVoist was an early Free Methodist in Michigan.

ERNY, Edward. Mission Accomplished. Under Sentence of Death: Life of Henry Steel. Westchester, Illinois: Good News Publishers, 1967. FMHC

FAIRBAIRN, Charles V. I Call to Remembrance. Winona Lake, Indiana: Light and Life Press, 1960. 185pp. FMHC RWC SAC

C. V. Fairbairn was the 17th Free Methodist Bishop. Autobiography.

GRIFFITH, Lillian. Living Embers; the Life and Writings of George William Griffith. Winona Lake, Indiana: Light and Life Press, c1937. 319pp. FMHC SPU RWC

G. W. Griffith was the 12th Free Methodist Bishop.

HAYWOOD, A. L. My Life Story. Stanwood, Michigan: By author, 195?. FMHC

Rev. Haywood was a pastor, District Elder and evangelist with the Free Methodist North Michigan and East Michigan Conferences.

HOGUE, Emma L. Adella Paulina Carpenter: In Memory of a
    Beautiful Life. Winona Lake, Indiana: Woman's Mis-
    sionary Society, 1939. 112pp. FMHC   RWC

Adella Carpenter taught at A. M. Chesbrough Seminary now
Roberts Wesleyan College for many years. She was active
in the early days of the Woman's Missionary Society and
was the editor of Missionary Tidings.

JOHNSTON, Tom and Roberta Johnston. Yesterday's Hate:
    Today's Love. The Amazing Story of Tom and Roberta
    Johnston. Winona Lake, Indiana: Light and Life Men
    International, 1974. FMHC

The Johnstons were in evangelistic crusades.

JONES, Burton Rensselaer. Incidents in the Life and Labors
    of Burton Rensselaer Jones, Minister of the Gospel with
    Extracts from His Diary. Chicago, Illinois: Free
    Methodist Publishing House, 1909. 316pp.
    FMHC   RWC   SPU

B. R. Jones was the 4th Free Methodist Bishop.

KYSOR, Kenneth. At Evening Time It Shall Be Light: Ben-
    jamin Titus Roberts and the Free Methodist Church.
    Cattaraugus, New York: By author, 1976. 48pp.
    FMHC   RWC   SPU

Compendium of miscellaneous information on B. T. Robert's
ancestors and relatives. Includes several verses by B. T.
Roberts.

LA DUE, John. The Life of Rev. Thomas Scott La Due, with
    some of his Sermon Sketches and other writings. Chicago,
    Illinois: Free Methodist Publishing House, 1898. 352pp.
    FMHC   RWC   SAC

This volume also contains a brief memoir of the wife of
Thomas La Due, Martha Kendall La Due by William La Due.

LEETE, Frederick De Land. Methodist Bishops: Personal
Notes and Bibliography. Nashville, Tennesee: Parthenon, 1948. FMHC RWC

Includes Free Methodist Bishops.

NELSON, Thomas H. Life and Labors of Rev. Vivian A. Dake:
Organizer and Leader of Pentecost Bands, embracing an
Account of his travels in America, Europe and Africa,
with selections from his Sketches, Poems, and Songs.
Chicago, Illinois: T. B. Arnold, 1894. FMHC

Rev. Dake is best known for his work with the Pentecost
Bands which are perhaps the forerunners of the present-day
Free Methodist VISA-VIA groups. (See also Parsons, Ida
Dake entry. Biography)

NISHIMURA, Kimi, ed. A Life Dedicated: Incidents in the
Life of a Home Missionary. Los Angeles, California:
Los Angeles Free Methodist Church, 1964. FMHC

Nishimura tells the story of Mrs. Laura Bodenhamer who
started Free Methodist work with the Pacific Coast Japanese in 1911.

OWEN, Epenetus. Struck by Lightning: A True and Thrill-
ing Narrative of one who was Struck by Lightning; with
incidents, Experiences, and Anecdotes, for old and
young. Cortland, New York: Cortland Co., 1878. FMHC

Early Free Methodist - contemporary of B. T. Roberts.

PARSONS, Ida Dake. Kindling Watch-Fires: Being a Brief
Sketch of the Life of Rev. Vivian A. Dake, Together
with a Compilation of Selections from his Writings,
Sermons, and Poems, to which is appended a few of His
Best Songs with Music. Chicago, Illinois: Free Meth-
odist Publishing House, 1915. FMHC

Written by the Wife of Rev. Dake (See also Nelson, Thomas
H. entry. Biography)

RAY, L. P. Twice Sold, Twice Ransomed: Autobiography
   of Mr. and Mrs. L. P. Ray. Chicago, Illinois: Free
   Methodist Publishing House, 1926. FMHC RWC

REDFIELD, John Wesley. Autobiography of John Wesley
   Redfield. Handwritten Manuscript. No. 82, Accession
   List. Free Methodist Historical Center

RHODES, M. L. Clifford B. Barrett: The "Happy Alleghen-
   ian." Chicago, Illinois: W. B. Rose, 1919. 192pp.
   FMHC RWC

Barrett was a preacher in Pittsburg and Oil City Conferences of the Free Methodist Church.

ROBERTS, Benson Howard. Benjamin Titus Roberts: A Biography. New York, New York: "The Earnest Christian"
   Office, 1900. 570pp. FMHC RWC SAC SPU

"The author, Benson Roberts, was the son of the Principal
founder of the Free Methodist Church, B. T. Roberts, who
served as its general superintendent (later called Bishop)
for a third of a century. During that period he edited
and published the periodical "The Earnest Christian," as
well as the official church publication "The Free Methodist." The son's account is a prime source of information
concerning the father's life and attainments."
L. R. Marston.

ROBERTS, Ellen Lois. Diary. Unpublished manuscript.
   Roberts Wesleyan College, 1839-1845; 1848-1953; 1857;
   1874-1875. RWC

ROBERTS, Esther Mae. The Bishop and His Lady. Winona
   Lake, Indiana: Light and Life Press, c1962. 104pp.
   FMHC RWC

Story of B. T. Roberts and his wife, Ellen Lois Roberts.
Written for teenagers.

SAGE, Charles H. Autobiography of Rev. Charles H. Sage.
   Embracing an account of his pioneer work in Michigan,

of the formation of the Canada Conference and of his
Labors in various States. W. B. Olmstead, ed. Chicago,
Illinois: Free Methodist Publishing House, 1903.
178pp.   FMHC   RWC   SAC

Rev. Sage was the first appointed Free Methodist pastor in
Canada.

SHAY, Emma Freeland. Mariet Hardy Freeland: A Faithful
    Witness. Chicago, Illinois: Free Methodist Publish-
    ing House, 1913. 244pp.   FMHC   RWC

Mrs. Freeland was one of the "Mothers of Free Methodism"
who lived in western New York at the time of the founding
of the Free Methodist Church. She pioneered in South
Dakota, helped found Wessington Springs Seminary and was
active in the early days of the General Women's Missionary
Society. She also wrote for the Earnest Christian and
Free Methodist magazines.

SHAY, Emma Freeland. Mariet Hardy Freeland: A Faithful
    Witness. 2nd ed. Chicago, Illinois: Free Methodist
    Publishing House, c1914. 224pp.   RWC

SHELHAMER, Ernest Ellsworth, ed. Life and Labors of Auntie
    Coon. Atlanta, Georgia: Repairer Office, 1905. 301pp.
    FMHC

Arvilla Damon Coon was a pioneer Free Methodist in the
Illinois area.

SHELHAMER, Ernest Ellsworth. Sixty Years of Thorns and
    Roses. Cincinnati, Ohio: God's Bible School Revival-
    ist, n.d.   FMHC

Life of E. E. Shelhamer, Free Methodist evangelist.

SHELHAMER, Ernest Ellsworth. A Spartan Evangel: Life
    Story of E. E. Shelhamer. Winona Lake, Indiana:
    Light and Life Press, 1951. 236pp.   FMHC   SAC

10

SHELHAMER, Ernest Ellsworth. The Ups and Downs of a Pioneer Preacher also some of my mistakes and what they
taught me. Atlanta, Georgia: Repairer Publishing
House, 1915. 272pp. FMHC RWC SAC

SHELHAMER, Julia A. Trials and Triumphs of a Minister's -
Wife. Atlanta, Georgia: Repairer Publishing Co., 1923.
FMHC

Personal experiences and the life story of the second wife
of E. E. Shelhamer, Free Methodist Evangelist.

SHOWERS, Mrs. Aura Claire. Rev. Aura Claire Showers: A
Sketch of his Life by his wife, together with Tributes
by Ministerial Bretheren to which is added a treatise
on the doctrine of Eternal Punishment and other unpublished manuscripts. North Chili, New York: Earnest
Christian Publishing House, 1896. FMHC

SMITH, Bertha B. and Julia A. Shelhamer. A Remarkable
Woman: The Life of Mrs. Minnie B. Shelhamer. 2nd ed.
Atlanta, Georgia: Repairer Publishing Co., n.d. FMHC

Biography of the first wife of E. E. Shelhamer.

SNYDER, H. A. "The Convicted Preacher (B. T. Roberts)."
Free Methodist, (May 24, 1966), p. 8. FMHC RWC SAC
SPU

B. T. Roberts, a founder of Free Methodism, founded Chili
Seminary (now Roberts Wesleyan College), urged establish-
ment of Spring Arbor College, encouraged the founding of
Greenville College and selected the site for the Seattle
Seminary (now Seattle Pacific University).

SNYDER, Lefa E. and Bernice E. Weidman. Servant of God:
Life Story and Selected Articles of Bishop Arthur D.
Zahniser. Winona Lake, Indiana: Light and Life Press,
c1940. 185pp. FMHC RWC

Arthur D. Zahniser was the 11th Free Methodist Bishop.

STEDWELL, Anson. Itinerant Footprints. Shambaugh, Iowa, 1915. 339pp. FMHC SAC

Rev. Stedwell was an itinerant pastor in the early days of Free Methodism in Illinois, Iowa, Nebraska, and the West Iowa Conferences.

TABOR, Mary. Puss. Winona Lake, Indiana: The Woman's Missionary Society, 1946. FMHC

History of the Free Methodist Mission in Kentucky. Puss is a cat!

TAMBLYN, Jeremiah W. Sweet Memories of a Trustful Life. By author, 1924. FMHC

Rev. Tamblyn was a pastor for many years in the New York Conference from its beginning and served most of its circuits.

TENNEY, Mary Alice. Adventure in Christian Love. Winona Lake, Indiana: Light and Life Press, 1964. 127pp. FMHC SAC

Short biographies on B. T. Roberts, Ellen Lois Roberts, Adella P. Carpenter, Grace Allen, Clara Leffingwell, Jennie La Due and the women of the Pentecost Bands.

TERRILL, Joseph Goodwin. The Life of Rev. John Wesley Redfield, M. D. Chicago, Illinois: Free Methodist Publishing House, 1889. FMHC

Dr. Redfield pioneered in the reform movement in Illinois before B. T. Roberts organized the Free Methodist Church in Western New York.

TERRILL, Joseph Goodwin. The Life of Rev. John Wesley Redfield. Chicago, Illinois: Free Methodist Publishing House, 1912. 464pp. SAC

TREVER, Robert. Life and Labors of Rev. Robert Trever
   both in England and America also a Sketch of Frontier
   Work in Connection with the Free Methodist Church with
   an Appendix Containing Temperance and other matter.
   St. Louis, Missouri: J. H. Flower Publishing House,
   1905. FMHC

Rev. Trever started the Free Methodist ministry in Nebraska. He writes on the organization of the West Kansas,
Oklahoma and Illinois Converences. Autobiography.

WARD, Ernest F. Memory Links of "Our Own Chickabiddie"
   or Reminiscences of Mary Louise Vore. Chicago, Illinois: Free Methodist Publishing House, n.d. FMHC
   RWC

WILLIAMSON, Glen. Julia, Giantess in Generosity: The
   Story of Julia Arnold Shelhamer. Winona Lake, Indiana:
   Light and Life Press, 1969. FMHC

WOOD, Levi. Life of Levi Wood. Unpublished Manuscript.
   No. 65, Documentary Record. Free Methodist Historical
   Center.

ZAHNISER, Clarence Howard. Earnest Christian: Life and
   Works of Benjamin Titus Roberts. n.p. 1957. 349pp.
   FMHC   RWC   SAC

BIOGRAPHY - Handbooks
(No locations given)

AMERICAN Men of Science: A Biographical Directory. New
York, New York: Bowker, 1906- .

DICTIONARY of American Biography. Dumas Malone, ed. New
York, New York: Charles Scribner's Sons, 1943.

LEADERS in Education: A Biographical Directory. Lancaster,
Pennsylvania: Science Press, 1932- .

WHO Was Who in Church History. Elgin S. Moyer, ed. Chicago, Illinois: Moody Press, 1962.

WHO Was Who in America: A Companion Volume to Who's Who.
Chicago, Illinois: Marquis, 1943- .

WHO's Who in Methodism. E. T. Clark, ed. Chicago, Illinois: Marquis, c1952. 860pp.

WHO's Who in America. Chicago, Illinois: Marquis.
Biennial.

WHO'S Who in Religion, 1975-1976. 1st ed. Chicago, Illinois: Marquis, 1975.

CATECHISM, DISCIPLINES, YEARBOOKS
(Organizational material)

CONSTITUTION of the Holiness Movement Church of the Evangelical Copts in the Arab Republic of Egypt. 1st ed.
Free Methodist Church, 1974.

Arabic-English typescript at Free Methodist Historical
Center.

DESIGN for Diligent Witness: Official Guidebook. Winona
    Lake, Indiana: Free Methodist Publishing House, 1961.
    RWC   (Free Methodist Youth)

FREE METHODIST Church of North America. Catechism of the
    Free Methodist Church. Free Methodist Publishing House,
    1902, 1920, 1954, 1957. FMHC   RWC

FREE METHODIST Church of North America. Digest of Free
    Methodist Law, or Guide in the Administration of the
    Discipline of the Free Methodist Church. Chicago,
    Illinois: Free Methodist Publishing House, 1901, 1908,
    1924, 1935. FMHC   RWC   SAC   SPU

FREE METHODIST Church of North America. Doctrines and
    Discipline, 1860-   . Buffalo; Rochester; Chicago;
    Winona Lake, Indiana. FMHC   RWC   SAC   SPU
    Quadrennial 1862-1955
    Quinquinnial 1955-

Now published as the Book of Discipline. Includes Constitution.

FREE METHODIST Church of North America. Doctrines and
    Discipline. Translated into Chinese by Miss. E. F.
    Jones, n.p., 1920. SPU

A translation in Japanese also exists.

FREE METHODIST Church of North America. Minutes of the
    General Conference. Unpublished Manuscript, 1862-
    1974. Free Methodist Historical Center.

FREE METHODIST Church. Women's Missionary Society. Con-
    stitution and By-Laws of the General Conference, Dis-
    trict, Local and Junior Societies. Free Methodist
    Publishing House, 1898-   . FMHC   RWC

FREE METHODIST Church. Woman's Missionary Society. Re-
    port of Meetings. Quadrennial. 1897?-   . FMHC   RWC

FREE METHODIST Church of North America. Yearbook.
Rochester; Winona Lake, Indiana: Free Methodist Pub-
lishing House, 1861-   . Annual. FMHC   RWC   SAC
SPU

Also published as combined Annual Conference Minutes.

Since 1970, the yearbook has been published in two volumes. Volume I contains information on personnel and the
organization, Volume II contains statistics. There are
three Free Methodist General Conferences in the world.
The Yearbook gives personnel and statistics for all the
General Conferences.

YOUNG MINISTER's Companion or a Collection of Valuable and
Scarce Treatises on the Pastoral Office. Boston, Massachusetts: n.p., 1813.   FMHC   SPU

This contains "Baxter's Reformed Pastor" from which the
Free Methodist Discipline quotes.

CHURCH MEMBERSHIP

BASTIAN, Donald N. The Mature Church Member. Pastor
Instruction Series. Adult Division. Winona Lake,
Indiana: Light and Life Press, 1963. 168pp.   FMHC
RWC   SAC   SPU

BASTIAN, Donald N. The Mature Church Member. rev. ed.
Winona Lake, Indiana: Light and Life Press, 1974.
FMHC   SPU

HASLAM, Robert B. FREE... Heritage of Faith and Life.
Winona Lake, Indiana: General Council for Church in
mission, 1973.   FMHC

No. 8 in "My Church" Series.

MARSTON, Leslie R. and others. My Church. Winona Lake,
Indiana: Free Methodist Publishing House, 1964. 31pp.
FMHC

MAVIS, Walter Curry. Advancing the Smaller Local Church.
Winona Lake, Indiana: Light and Life Press, 1957.
189pp. FMHC   RWC   SAC

NELSON, Royal S. Here's the Answer: A Handbook for Sunday
School Workers. Winona Lake, Indiana: Light and Life
Press, 1963. FMHC   RWC

OLMSTEAD, B. L. Leader's Guide to the Meaning of Church
Membership. Winona Lake, Indiana: Light and Life
Press, n.d. FMHC

OLMSTEAD, B. L. Our Church at Work: A Brief Manual for
the Instruction of Preparatory Members of the Free
Methodist Church. Free Methodist Publishing House,
n.d. RWC

WATSON, C. Hoyt. Advancing Church Membership. Pastor
Instruction Series. Youth Division. Winona Lake,
Indiana: Free Methodist Publishing House, n.d.
FMHC   SPU

WATSON, C. Hoyt. Exploring Church Membership. Pastor
Instruction Series. Junior Division. Winona Lake,
Indiana, n.d.   FMHC   SPU

WATSON, C. Hoyt. The Fragrance of My Church. Winona
Lake, Indiana: Forward Movement, n.d. 8pp.   FMHC

WATSON, C. Hoyt. The Free Methodist Church – Its Mission,
Its Doctrines, Its Standards. Winona Lake, Indiana:
Forward Movement, n.d. 8pp.   FMHC

WHAT is a Free Methodist? Winona Lake, Indiana: General
Council for Church in Mission, 1972.   FMHC

No. 1 in "My Church" Series.

ALLAN, David. From the Lumber Camp to the Ministry: The Autobiography of Rev. David Allan. 1st ed. Toronto, Ontario: Evangelical Publishers, 1939. FMHC

Historical information on the West Ontario Conference.

ATKINSON, Donald L. A Study of Methods used in the Establishment and Growth of Selected Churches in the Pacific Northwest Conference of the Free Methodist Church. Unpublished M.A. thesis, Seattle Pacific College, 1970. SPU

BROOKS, Philip F. The History of the Pacific Northwest Conference of the Free Methodist Church. Unpublished Master of Divinity thesis, Western Evangelical Seminary, 1969. FMHC

Bibliography, pp. 133-140. Bibliography includes numerous citations on Free Methodist institutions in the Pacific Northwest including Warm Beach Manor (retirement home) and Warm Beach Campgrounds.

DeVOIST, M. History of the East Michigan Conference of the Free Methodist Church. Owosso, Michigan: By author, 1925. 552pp. FMHC SAC

EAST MICHIGAN CONFERENCE. Historical Sketches of the Free Methodist Churches of the East Michigan Conference, 1924-1962. Jessie R. Booth, ed. Linden, Michigan: By author, 1963. 163pp. FMHC SAC

EAST ONTARIO CONFERENCE: 1895-1970 - 75 Years of Progress in Canadian Free Methodism. n.p., 1970. FMHC

EAST ONTARIO CONFERENCE. Focus on Gains. n.p., 1966. 11pp. FMHC

GENESEE CONFERENCE. Genesee Conference History, Free Methodist Church: 1860-1959. From Age to Age the Same Message. Wesley R. Wilder, et. al., ed. 1958 FMHC

GENESEE CONFERENCE. History of Genesee Conference Woman's
    Missionary Society of the Free Methodist Church, 1895-
    1945. Lena A. Southworth, comp. n.p., 1946? RWC

MAVIS, Marion. A Brief Story of the Kentucky-Tennessee
    Conference, written for the 75th Anniversary Commemora-
    tion. Wilmore, Kentucky, 1970. 23pp. FMHC

Cover-title: In the beginning; a history of the Free Methodist Church in Kentucky-Tennessee from its earliest beginnings until 1970.

MAYNARD, J. Louise. God's Lamp: History of the Central
    Illinois Conference Free Methodist Church. Greenville,
    Illinois: Tower Press, 1960. FMHC

"Centennial Anniversary Souvenir History."

MOTTWEILER, Evelyn L. "They Started 100 Years Ago." Light
    and Life, (September 21, 1976), p. 8. FMHC   RWC   SAC
    SPU

On North Michigan Conference and Free Methodism in Canada.

NELSON, Walter O. A History of the Oklahoma Annual Confer-
    ence of the Free Methodist Church of North America.
    Siloam Springs, Arkansas: Silent Minister Booket Press,
    1949. 36pp. FMHC

OIL CITY CONFERENCE. Our Heritage, 1898-1973. R. R. Blews
    and Frances McKay Roggenbaum, ed's., 1973. 95pp.
    FMHC   RWC

Includes History on the Oil City Conference Northwestern
Pennsylvania.

NEW YORK CONFERENCE. The Vision Glorious. Sept. 2-6,
    1874, Brooklyn, New York: Sept. 26-28, 1974, Beach
    Lake, Pennsylvania. Winona Lake, Indiana: Light and
    Life Press, 1974. FMHC

History of New York Conference.

STEDWELL, Anson. Itinerant Footprints. Shambaugh, Iowa, n.p., 1915. FMHC

Information on the West Iowa Conference.

SUSQUEHANNA CONFERENCE. History, 1862-1960. Philip E. Myette, comp. n.p., n.d. FMHC

TEXAS CONFERENCE. Its Origin and Present Churches, Published in Observance of its 80th Anniversary, 1881-1960, n.p., 1960. FMHC

TREVER, Robert. Life and Labors of Rev. Robert Trever both in England and America also a Sketch of Frontier Work in Connection with the Free Methodist Church with an Appendix containing Temperance and other matter. Autobiography. St. Louis, Missouri: J. H. Flower, 1905. FMHC

Historical information on organization of West Kansas Conference and also in Oklahoma and Illinois.

WEST ONTARIO CONFERENCE. 1895-1945, 50 Years of Progress: Golden Anniversary. n.p., 1945. FMHC

YAMADA, Miyoko. The Pacific Coast Japanese Conference of the Free Methodist Church. Unpublished Master of Religious Education thesis, Fuller Theological Seminary, 1966. FMHC

ZAHNISER, Arthur and John B. Easton. History of the Pittsburgh Conference of the Free Methodist Church. Chicago, Illinois: Free Methodist Publishing House, 1932. 355pp. FMHC RWC

CONFERENCE - Newsletters

✗ATLANTIC SOUTHEAST CONFERENCE. Vanguard. 1- , ?- . Murphy, North Carolina. FMHC

20

✗CALIFORNIA CONFERENCE. The Conference Echoes. 1- , 1947- .
   Modesto, California.   FMHC

Monthly for 10 months.

CANADA EAST. Advance. 1- , 1964- . Belleville, Ontario.
   FMHC

Quarterly.

CANADA WEST. Voice of Canada West. 1- , 1962- . Moose
   Jaw, Sask.   FMHC

Bi-monthly.

✗CENTRAL ILLINOIS CONFERENCE. Central Illinois Booster.
   1- , 1943- . Greenville, Illinois.   FMHC

1943-1965 Monthly.
1966-   Bi-monthly.

✗ CENTRAL ILLINOIS CONFERENCE. The Conference Gleaner. 1- ,
   1966- . Greenville, Illinois.   FMHC

Weekly.

✗CENTENARY CONFERENCE. Challenger. 1- , 1960- . Sara-
   toga Springs, New York York.   FMHC

Bi-monthly. Monthly to 1976.

✗EAST MICHIGAN CONFERENCE. The Voice of the East Michigan
   Conference. 1- , 1947- . Flint, Michigan.   FMHC
   ?-? as The Voice of Your Church of the East Michigan
   Conference.

Monthly for 10 months.

GENESEE CONFERENCE. Genesee Conference News. 1- ,
    ?- . North Chili, New York. FMHC RWC

ILLINOIS-WISCONSIN CONFERENCE. Messenger. 1- , 1966- .
    Woodstock, Illinois. FMHC

Monthly for 10 months.
Wisconsin Conference News merged with Illinois Messenger.

IOWA CONFERENCE. Iowa Conference Messenger. 1- , 1943- .
    Des Moines, Iowa. FMHC

Monthly. ?-1963 as The West Iowan (before Conference
merger).

KANSAS CONFERENCE. Kansas Conference Newsletter. 1-?,
    ?-1972. McPherson, Kansas. FMHC

KANSAS CONFERENCE. The Superintendent's Scoop. 1- ,
    1968- . McPherson, Kansas. FMHC

KENTUCKY, TENNESEE. Pastoral Newsletter. 1- , 1966- .
    Scottsville, Kentucky. FMHC

Also published as Newslink, Builder.

LOUISIANA CONFERENCE. Louisiana Messenger. 1- , 1935 - .
    Alexandria, Louisiana. FMHC

Monthly.

MARYLAND-VIRGINIA CONFERENCE. Conference News-Herald.
    1- , 1944. Spencerville, Maryland. FMHC

MINN-I-KOTA CONFERENCE. Life-style. 1- , 1976- .
    Bloomington, Minnesota. FMHC

1965-1970 as Super-vision.
1970-1972 as Sharing.

NEBRASKA CONFERENCE. Nebraska Conference Advance. 1- ,
1963- . Lincoln, Nebraska.

?-? as Missouri Messenger.

NEW YORK CONFERENCE. New York Conference News. 1- , ?- .
South Canaan, Pennsylvania. FMHC

NORTH MICHIGAN CONFERENCE. North Michigan Herald. 1- ,
1956- . Big Rapid, Michigan. FMHC

?-? as The Conference Herald.
Monthly except July.

OHIO CONFERENCE. Ohio Conference News. 1- , ?- .
Columbus, Ohio. FMHC

OIL CITY CONFERENCE. Oil City Conference News. 1- ,
1946- . Pleasantville, Pennsylvania. FMHC

?-? as The Illuminator.
Published 10 months of the year.

OKLAHOMA CONFERENCE. Oklahoma Free Methodist. 1- ,
1963- . Midwest City, Oklahoma. FMHC

v.1- ?, 1952-1963 as Oklahoma Conference Clarion.

OREGON CONFERENCE. Oregon Conference News. 1- , ?- .
Turner, Oregon. FMHC

OZARK CONFERENCE. Ozark Conference Echo. 1- , ?- .
Jefferson City, Missouri. FMHC

PACIFIC COAST JAPANESE CONFERENCE. No regular conference
news bulletin.

PACIFIC NORTHWEST CONFERENCE. Conference News. 1- ,
    1963- . Seattle, Washington. FMHC

1945-1963 as Washington Conference News.
10 issues per year.

PITTSBURGH CONFERENCE. Pittsburgh Conference Herald.
    1- , ?- . Apolla, Pennsylvania. FMHC

ROCKY MOUNTAIN CONFERENCE. Rocky Mountain Conference
    Messenger. v. 1. , ?- . Denver, Colorado. FMHC

SOUTHERN CALIFORNIA-ARIZONA CONFERENCE. Southern Califor-
    nia-Arizona Conference Observer. 1- , 1961- . Glen-
    dora, California. FMHC

Bi-monthly.

SOUTHERN MICHIGAN CONFERENCE. The Vision. 1- , 1945- .
    Spring Arbor, Michigan. FMHC

?-? as The Michigan Vision.
Monthly.

SUSQUEHANNA CONFERENCE. Susquehanna Advance. 1- , 1960- .
    Syracuse, New York. FMHC

?-1960 as Susquehanna Challenger.

TEXAS CONFERENCE. Texas Conference News Letter. 1- ,
    1936- . Atascosa, Texas. FMHC

Also published as The Beacon Light, 1936-1960.
Monthly.

WABASH CONFERENCE. Wabash Courier. 1- , 1945- .
    Indianapolis, Indiana. FMHC

Monthly.

DEVOTIONAL WORKS AND PRACTICE OF THE CHRISTIAN LIFE

BALDWIN, Harmon A. The Fisherman of Galilee: A Devotional
    Study of the Apostle Peter. New York: Fleming H.
    Revell, 1923. 160pp. FMHC

BANKS, Stanley. Saints in Work Clothes. Winona Lake,
    Indiana: Light and Life Press, 1975. 188 pp. FMHC

BARTLETTE, William Henry. Etchics Real or Relative? An
    Inquiry into the Place of Christianity in World Ethical
    Philosophies. (An Outline Survey in Layman's Language.)
    New York, New York: Vantage Press, 1971. FMHC

CHILDREN'S Edition of Touching Incidents and Remarkable
    Answers to Prayer. S. B. Shaw, comp. Guthrie, Okla-
    homa: Faith Publishing House, c1895, 1968. FMHC

DEMARAY, Donald E. Alive to God Through Prayer: A Manual
    on the Practices of Prayer. Winona Lake, Indiana:
    Light and Life Press, c1965. 156pp. FMHC RWC

DYING Testimonies of Saved and Unsaved. Gathered from
    Authentic Sources. S. B. Shaw, comp. Noblesville,
    Indiana: Newby Book Room, c1898, 1969. FMHC

FINE, Robert M. Great Today's, Better Tomorrows. Winona
    Lake, Indiana: Light and Life Press, 1976. FMHC RWC

GRIFFITH, George W. Daily Glow. Mr. G. W. Griffith, comp.
    Winona Lake, Indiana: Light and Life Press, c1941,
    1952. FMHC RWC

George W. Griffith was the 12th Free Methodist bishop.

GRIFFITH, George W. Lest We Forget: Selected Messages by
    George W. Griffith. Mrs. G. W. Griffith, comp. Los
    Angeles, California: By compiler. c1939. FMHC

HARVEY, J. D. Dimensions in Christian Living. Winona
    Lake, Indiana: Light and Life Press, 1973.   FMHC

HARVEY, J. D. Faith Plus: Search for the Holy Life.
    Winona Lake, Indiana: Light and Life Press, 1976.
    FMHC

HOGUE, Wilson Thomas. The Class-Meeting as a Means of
    Grace. Chicago, Illinois: S. K. J. Chesbrough, 1907.
    168pp.   FMHC   RWC   SAC

Wilson T. Hogue was the 6th Free Methodist Bishop.

HOWELL, Roy W. Christian Family; a Symposium. Winona
    Lake, Indiana: Light and Life Press, c1965. 137pp.
    FMHC   RWC

Includes Bibliographies.

HOWELL, Roy Wilbur. Saved to Serve; Accent on Steward-
    ship. Winona Lake, Indiana: Light and Life Press,
    1965. 132pp.   FMHC   RWC

Bibliography, pp. 131-132.

HOWLAND, Jenne Harroun. Not Mine. Winona Lake, Indiana:
    Woman's Missionary Society: Free Methodist Publishing
    House, 1947. 154pp.   FMHC   RWC

HUMPHREY, J. M. The Convert's Homeward Guide. Chicago,
    Illinois: W. B. Rose, 1916. 126pp.   FMHC

HUMPHREY, J. M. Crumbs from Heaven. Chicago, Illinois:
    Light and Life Press, 1927.   FMHC

KNOX, Lloyd H., et. al. A Faith to Grow By. Winona Lake,
    Indiana: Light and Life Press, 1977. 96pp.   FMHC

26

LOWELL, LeRoy M. Building the House Beautiful: A Study
in Personal Religious Living. Winona Lake, Indiana:
Light and Life Press, c1939. 77pp. FMHC RWC

MARSTON, Leslie Ray. From Chaos to Character: A Study in
the Stewardship of Personality. Suggestions for Study
by Lois Wood-Woods. Greenville, Illinois: Tower Press,
1935. 175pp. FMHC RWC SAC SPU

MARSTON, Leslie Ray. From Chaos to Character: A Study in
the Stewardship of Personality. Study Suggestions and
Worship Guide by Lois Wood-Woods. 2nd ed. Greenville,
. Illinois: Tower Press, 1937. 192pp. FMHC RWC

MARSTON, Leslie Ray. From Chaos to Character: A Study in
the Stewardship of Personality. Study Suggestions and
Worship Guide by Lois Wood-Woods. 3rd ed. Winona Lake,
Indiana: Light and Life Press, 1944. 192pp. FMHC RWC

MAVIS. W. Curry. Beyond Conformity. Winona Lake, Indiana:
Light and Life Press, 1958. 160pp. FMHC RWC SAC

"Evangelical concepts of Christian experience, Christian
objectives and methods of advancing the kingdom of God."
p. 1. W. C. Mavis.

MAVIS. W. Curry. The Holy Spirit in the Christian Life.
Winona Lake, Indiana: Light and Life Press, 1977.
146pp. FMHC

MAVIS, W. Curry. Personal Renewal through Christian Conversion. Kansas City, Missouri: Beacon Hill Press of
Kansas City, 1969. FMHC RWC

MAVIS. W. Curry. The Psychology of Christian Experience.
Grand Rapids, Michigan: Zondervan Publishing House,
1963. 155pp. RWC SAC FMHC

McKENNA, David L. Awake My Conscience! Winona Lake,
Indiana: Light and Life Press, 1977. 128 pp. FMHC

OLMSTEAD, B. L. Being a Christian. n.p.,n.d., 32pp. FMHC

ROBERTS, Benjamin Titus. First Lessons on Money. Rochester, New York, 1886. 160pp. FMHC RWC SAC SPU

SHAW, S.B. God's Financial Plan or Temporal Prosperity, the Result of Faithful Stewardship. Chicago, Illinois: S.B. Shaw, 1897. 296pp. FMHC

SHELHAMER, Julia A. A Message to Men with Closing Appeal by Her Husband. Kansas City, Missouri: Nazarene Publishing House and Atlanta, Georgia: Repairer Publishing Company, n.d. FMHC

SIMS, Arthur. Bible Salvation and Popular Religion Contrasted. Kingston, Ontario, Canada: By author, 1886. 4th ed. FMHC

SIMS, Arthur. Grace and Glory or Godly Counsel and Encouragement for Waiting, Watching Hearts. Chicago, Illinois: W. B. Rose, n.d. FMHC

SIMS, Albert. Remarkable Narratives; or, Records of Powerful Revivals, Striking Providences, Wonderful Religious Experience, Tragic Death-bed Scenes, and other Authentic Incidents, to which is added some Valuable Hints for Christian Workers. Kingston, Ontario: By author, 1896. 352pp. FMHC

SIMS, Albert. Remarkable Narratives....Pittsburg, Pennsylvania: Hogue and Co., 1902. 352pp. FMHC

SPIRITUAL Renewal for Methodism: A Discussion of the Early Methodist Class Meeting and the Values Inherent in Personal Groups Today. Nashville, Tennessee: Methodist Evangelistic Materials, 1958. FMHC

One chapter is by Dr. Mary Alice Tenney, Greenville College.

TENNEY, Mary Alice. Blueprint for a Christian World: An
    Analysis of the Wesleyan Way. Winona Lake, Indiana:
    Light and Life Press, 1953. 292pp. FMHC RWC SAC

TENNEY, Mary Alice. Living in Two Worlds: How a Christian
    does it! Winona Lake, Indiana: Light and Life Press,
    1958. 118pp. FMHC RWC SAC

TURNER, George. "The Holy Life," Free Methodist. (Octo-
    ber 10, 1967), p. 16. FMHC RWC SAC SPU

WARREN, R. Barclay. You Can Gain Spiritual Strength.
    Toronto, Ontario, Canada: Thomas Nelson, 1963. FMHC
    RWC

WARREN, R. Barclay. Spiritual Strength for Today. Toronto,
    Ontario, Canada: Thomas Nelson, 1955. FMHC

WHITCOMB, A. L. Emmanuel and Stepping Stones to Union
    with God. Winona Lake, Indiana: Light and Life Press,
    n.d. 93pp. FMHC

WINSLOW, Carolyn V. Forward With Christ. Winona Lake,
    Indiana: Young Peoples' Missionary Society, 1947. FMHC

DOCTRINAL WORKS BY FREE METHODIST AUTHORS

BALDWIN, Harmon Allen. The Carnal Mind: A Doctrinal and
    Experimental View of the Subject. Chicago, Illinois:
    Free Methodist Publishing House, 1926. 183pp. FMHC
    RWC

BALDWIN, Harmon Allen. Holiness and the Human Element.
    Louisville, Kentucky: Pentecostal Publishing Company,
    1919. 123pp. FMHC SAC

29

BALDWIN, Harmon Allen. Holiness and the Human Element.
2nd ed. Kansas City, Missouri: Nazarene Publishing
House, c1919, 1952. 110pp. FMHC

BALDWIN, Harmon Allen. The Indwelling Christ. Vander-
grift Heights, Pennsylvania: By author, 1912. 282pp.
FMHC   SAC

BALDWIN, Harmon Allen. Lessons for Seekers of Holiness.
Containing numerous quotations from Wesley, Fletcher,
and other standard authors, and designed to aid such
as are groaning after purity of heart in entering upon
the experience. Chicago, Illinois: S. K. J. Chesbrough, 1907. 180pp. FMHC   RWC   SAC

BALDWIN, Harmon Allen. Objections to Entire Sanctification Considered. Pittsburgh, Pennsylvania: By author,
1911. 63pp. FMHC   SAC

BASTIAN, Donald and Leslie R. Marston. Thumb-nail Sketches of Doctrinal Patterns. Winona Lake, Indiana:
Light and Life Press, n.d. 8pp. FMHC

Donald Bastian is the 24th Free Methodist Bishop and L. R.
Marston was the 15th.

BASTIAN, Donald. "What Does Our Church Believe About the
Bible?" Light and Life, (October 21, 1975), pp. 7-9.
FMHC   RWC   SAC   SPU

BATES, Gerald E. A Comparative Study of Calvin's and
Wesley's Conceptions of the Perfectibility of Man.
Unpublished Th.M. dissertation, Western Theological
Seminary, 1964. FMHC

DEMARAY, Donald E. Basic Beliefs: An Introductory Guide
to Christian Theology. Winona Lake, Indiana: Light
and Life Press, c1958, 1966. 140pp. FMHC   RWC

DEMARAY, Donald, et. al. We Believe. Winona Lake, Indiana: Light and Life Press, 1976. FMHC

Compilation of articles from the Light and Life magazine on the Free Methodist Articles of Faith.

EASTON, J. B. The Baptism and Indwelling of the Holy Ghost. Chicago, Illinois: Light and Life Press, n.d. FMHC RWC

FAIRBAIRN, Charles V. Purity and Power or The Baptism with the Holy Ghost. Chicago, Illinois: Christian Witness, 1930. FMHC

FAIRBAIRN, Charles V. What We Believe. Winona Lake, Indiana: Light and Life Press, 1957. FMHC RWC

FAITH and Life of a Free Methodist. Lloyd H. Knox, ed. Winona Lake, Indiana: Light and Life Press, 1976. FMHC SPU

"Approved and commended by the Study Commission on Doctrine: The Bishops with George L. Ford, Lyle E. Williams, Lloyd H. Knox and Jack H. Mottweiler, secretary." (from title page)

FURTHER Insights into Holiness. Nineteen leading Wesleyan Scholars Present Various Phases of Holiness Thinking. Kenneth Geiger, comp. Kansas City, Missouri. Beacon Hill Press, c1963, 1966. FMHC

Includes several Free Methodist Scholars.

GRIFFITH, George W. The Divine Program: An Interpretation of the Divine Method of Redemption and of the Nature and Nurture of the Christian Life. Chicago, Illinois: W. B. Rose, 1923. 256pp. FMHC RWC

GUIDE to Holiness. H. V. Degen and B. W. Corham, ed's. Boston, Massachusetts: Henvy V. Degen, c1857. 188pp. RWC

HAWKINS, Richard Watson. Life Eternal. Earnest Christian Printing, 1880.

HAWKINS, Richard Watson. Redemption, or the Living Way: A Treatise on the Redemption of the Body, including a Doctrinal Outline of Experimental Religion. Olean, New York: Herald Publishing House, 1888. 497pp. FMHC

HOGG, Wilson Thomas. A Symposium of Scriptural Holiness. Chicago, Illinois: Free Methodist Publishing House, 1896. 150pp. FMHC SAC SPU (Same as "Hogue")

Includes "Holiness not understood" by B. T. Roberts.

HOGUE, Wilson Thomas. The Believer's Personal Experience of Christ in the Process of Salvation. Chicago, Illinois: W. B. Rose, 1915. 58pp. FMHC SAC

HOGUE, Wilson Thomas. The Holy Spirit, a Study. Chicago, Illinois: W. B. Rose, 1916. 408pp. FMHC SAC

HOWLAND, Carl L. Proofs of Inspiration: the Cumulative Proofs of the Inspiration of the Scriptures. Free Methodist Publishing House, 1940. 58pp. FMHC

INSIGHTS into Holiness. Discussions of Holiness by Fifteen Leading Scholars of the Wesleyan Persuasion. Kansas City, Missouri: Beacon Hill Press, c1962, 1966. FMHC

JOY, Donald Marvin. The Holy Spirit and You. Winona Lake, Indiana: Light and Life Press, 1965. 187pp. FMHC RWC SAC

KING, Caroll Wesley, Jr. Infant Baptism in Biblical and Wesleyan Theology. Unpublished Thesis, Asbury Theological Seminary, 1975. FMHC

KNOX, Lloyd H. "How Does Sanctification Relate to Christian Witness and Service." Light and Life, (April 25, 1972), p. 5. FMHC RWC SAC SPU

LAMSON, Byron S.   The Holiness Teachings of New Testament
    Literature. Winona Lake, Indiana: Light and Life,
    n.d. 60pp.   FMHC

LINICOME, Forman. The Soul. Winona Lake, Indiana:
    Light and Life Press, 1940. 64 pp.   FMHC

LINICOME, Forman. The Three D's of the Sanctified.
    Winona Lake, Indiana: Light and Life Press, n.d. 63pp.
    FMHC

LINICOME, Forman. What is Your Life? Chicago, Illinois:
    Light and Life Press, 1933. 64pp.   FMHC

MARSTON, Leslie R. "Perspective: Bishop Roberts and
    Christian Holiness." Light and Life, (July 10, 1973),
    p. 15.   FMHC   RWC   SAC   SPU

MINISTERS' CONFERENCE of Greenville College, Greenville,
    Illinois, 12th, 1939. The Wesleyan Message: Its
    Scriptures and Historical Basis; Addresses Delivered
    at the 12th Annual Ministers' Conference, April 10-14,
    1939. Winona Lake, Indiana: Light and Life Press,
    1940. 220pp.   FMHC   RWC

MINISTERS' CONFERENCE of Greenville College, Greenville,
    Illinois, 13th-14th, 1940-1941. The Wesleyan Message
    Bearing Fruit; Addresses Delivered at the 13th and 14th
    sessions of the Ministers' Conference of Greenville
    College, April, 1940-1941. Winona Lake, Indiana:
    Light and Life Press, 1942. 174pp.   FMHC   SAC

OLMSTEAD, B. L. Three Types of Eternal Security. n.p.,
    n.d. 32pp.   FMHC

OWEN, Epenetus. Things New and Old. Boston, Massachu-
    setts: Henry V. Degen, c1855, 1856.   FMHC

PARSONS, Elmer E. Witness to the Resurrection. Winona
    Lake, Indiana: Light and Life, 1967.   FMHC

PEARCE, William. Our Incarnate Lord. Chicago, Illinois:

Light and Life Press, n.d. 144pp. FMHC RWC

RILEY, J. M. "The Holiness We Preach." Free Methodist,
(July 19, 1966), p. 10. FMHC RWC SAC SPU

ROBERTS, Benjamin Titus. Holiness Teachings, compiled from
the Editorial Writings of the late Rev. Benjamin T.
Roberts. North Chili, New York: "Earnest Christian"
Publishing House, c1893. 256pp. FMHC RWC SAC SPU

Examines holiness from all perspectives - properties,
nature, attributes, limits of sanctification.

ROBERTS, Benjamin Titus. Living Truths. E. D. Riggs, ed.
Winona Lake, Indiana: Light and Life Press, 1960.
FMHC RWC SAC SPU

Taken from Pungent Truths.

ROBERTS, Benjamin Titus. Pungent Truths; being Extracts
from the Writings of the Rev. Benjamin Titus Roberts.
William B. Rose, ed. Chicago, Illinois: Free Methodist Publishing House, 1912. 379pp. FMHC RWC SAC
SPU

SHELHAMER, Elmer Ellsworth. Bible Holiness, How Obtained,
How Retained. Chicago, Illinois: Free Methodist Publishing House, n.d. FMHC

SHELHAMER, Elmer Ellsworth. False Doctrines and Fanati-
cism Exposed. Atlanta, Georgia: "The Repairer," n.d.
128pp. FMHC SAC

SHELHAMER, Elmer Ellsworth. Popular and Radical Holiness,
Contrasted. Atlanta, Georgia: n.p., 1906. 159pp.
FMHC SAC

SIMS, Albert. Bible Salvation and Popular Religion Contrasted. 4th ed. Kingston, Ontario: By author, 1886.
FMHC

SIMS, Albert. Valuable Bank Notes; or, God's Immutable
    Promises, Searched, Tested and Found True. Toronto,
    Ontario: By author, 1902. 85pp. FMHC

SMASHEY, David Morton. The Redeeming Purpose of God.
    Including a Statement of the Scriptural Idea of the
    Doctrine of Holiness and Its Advancement in the Church.
    By author, 1913. Reprinted, 1970. FMHC

TAYLOR, Jesse Paul. Holiness, the Finished Foundation.
    Winona Lake, Indiana: Light and Life Press, c1963.
    216pp. FMHC   RWC   SAC   SPU

Jesse Paul Taylor was the 18th Free Methodist Bishop.

TAYLOR, Jesse Paul. The Music of Pentecost. Winona Lake,
    Indiana: Light and Life Press, 1951. 123pp. FMHC
    RWC   SAC

TURNER, George Allen. The More Excellent Way: the Scrip-
    tural Basis of the Wesleyan Message. Winona Lake,
    Indiana: Light and Life Press, 1952. 292pp. FMHC
    RWC   SAC

TURNER, George Allen. The Vision Which Transforms: Is
    Christian Perfection Scriptural? Kansas City, Missouri:
    Beacon Hill Press, 1964. FMHC   RWC

VAN VALIN, H. Frank. "Holiness is Wholeness." Light and
    Life, (March 9, 1971), p. 15. FMHC   SPU

WARNER, David Snethen. The Anointing of the Holy Spirit.
    Chicago, Illinois: Light and Life Press, 1925. 64pp.
    FMHC

David Warner was the 10th Free Methodist Bishop.

WHEATLAKE, S. K. Does the Bible Teach a Sinning Religion?
    n.p., n.d. FMHC

WHITEMAN, John H.   Amen, Hallelujah. Chicago, Illinois:
    W. B. Rose, n.d. 62pp.   FMHC   RWC

WISEMAN, Peter. Purity and Power or Sanctification at
    Pentecost. Chicago, Illinois: Christian Witness,
    n.d. FMHC

WISEMAN, Peter. Scriptural Sanctification. Kansas City,
    Missouri: Beacon Hill Press, 1951.   FMHC

WOOD, John Allen. Perfect Love; or, plain things for
    those who need them concerning the Doctrine, Experience,
    Profession and Practice of Christian Holiness. Rev.
    and enlarged ed. Chicago, Illinois: W. B. Rose, 1909.
    331pp. FMHC

WORD and the Doctrine. Studies in Contemporary Wesleyan-
    Arminian Theology. Kenneth E. Geiger, comp. Kansas
    City, Missouri: Beacon Hill Press, c1965.   FMHC

Several Free Methodist authors included.

EDUCATION - Free Methodist Educational Institutions -
                History

ALDERSGATE

BROWN, Zella Nixon. Aldersgate: The College of the Warm
    Heart. n.p., 1976.   FMHC

GREENVILLE COLLEGE

MILLER, Donald G. A History of Greenville College with
    Special Reference to the Curriculum. Unpublished.
    M.A. thesis, New York University, 1934. 126pp.

TENNEY, Mary Alice. Still Abides the Memory. Greenville,
    Illinois: Tower Press of Greenville College, 1942.
    322pp.   FMHC   SAC   SPU

LOS ANGELES PACIFIC COLLEGE (merged with Azusa College, now Azusa Pacific College)

GOODHEW, Edna F. Echoes from Half a Century. Los Angeles, California: Los Angeles Pacific College Press, 1960. 322pp. FMHC

ROBERTS WESLEYAN COLLEGE (Chili Seminary, A. M. Chesbrough Seminary, Roberts Junior College).

BACKENSTOE, Martin John. Triumphant Living: A Steward-ship Report. Kutztown, Pennsylvania: Kutztown Publishing Co., 1949. FMHC

Includes historical information on Chili Seminary.

MOORE, Carl C. Jr. Hidden Strands from the Fabric of Early Chili. n.p., 1976. 151pp. FMHC

Contains references to the history of the founding of Roberts Wesleyan College.

PFOUTS, Neil Edward. A History of Roberts Wesleyan College. Unpublished Master of Education thesis, University of Rochester, 1950. FMHC RWC

ROBERTS, Sellew. "A Centennial - The First Hundred Years." Free Methodist, (August 16, 1966), p. 1. FMHC RWC SAC SPU

Article relates to the historical progress of Roberts Wesleyan College. Includes a biography of B. T. Roberts.

SEATTLE PACIFIC UNIVERSITY (Seattle Seminary, Seattle Pacific College)

BEERS, Adelaide Lionne. The Romance of a Consecrated Life. A Biography of Alexander Beers. Chicago, Illinois: Free Methodist Publishing House, n.d. FMHC SPU

PETERSON, Mattie J. Footprints in the Sands of Time. n.p., 1960.

Early history of the Nils B. Peterson family including information on Seattle Seminary.

SPRING ARBOR COLLEGE.

KILLION, Mead Wilbur. A History of Spring Arbor Seminary and Junior College. Unpublished M. A. thesis, University of Michigan, 1941. SAC

SNYDER, Howard A. One Hundred Years at Spring Arbor. A History of Spring Arbor College, 1873-1973. Spring Arbor, Michigan: Spring Arbor College, 1973. 204pp. FMHC   SAC

Bibliography: p. (198)-204.

WESSINGTON SPRINGS

WALLER, Fred L. A History of Wessington Spring College. Unpublished M. A. thesis, University of South Dakota, Vermillion, 1935. 120pp.

EDUCATION - General Works related to Free Methodism.

BOWNES, Leona K. A Study of the Christian Day School Movement in the Arizona-Southern California Conference of the Free Methodist Church. Unpublished M. A. thesis, Seattle Pacific College, 1962. 113pp. SPU

FREE METHODIST Church. Commission on Christian Education. The Study of Free Methodist Higher Education. David L. McKenna, director. n.p., 1962. FMHC

"FREE METHODIST Higher Education," Light and Life, (May 18, 1976), pp. 10-11. FMHC   RWC   SAC   SPU

HERRON, Orley R. "Higher Education and the Church," Light and Life (August 25, 1970), p. 14. FMHC   RWC   SAC SPU

JOY, Donald Marvin. The Effects of the Value-Oriented Instruction in the Church and in the Home. Unpublished dissertation, Indiana University, 1969. FMHC

JOY, Donald, et. al. Let's Teach; Authorized by the Commission on Christian Education of the Free Methodist Church; Prepared by the Members of the Publishing House Staff. Winona Lake, Indiana: Light and Life Press, 1961. 123pp. SAC FMHC

MASON, Harold Carlton. Abiding Values in Christian Education. Westwood, New Jersey: F. H. Revell Co., 1955. 176pp. RWC FMHC

MCKENNA, David Loren. "Free Methodist Education - 1992." Free Methodist, (October 10, 1967), p. 23. FMHC RWC SAC SPU

NELSON, Marven O. "The Administration of Guidance in Colleges Related to the Wesleyan and Free Methodist Churches." Unpublished Ed. D. dissertation, University of Buffalo, 1952. RWC

PITTS, Robert Duane. A Comparative Environmental Study of Four Denominational Colleges. Unpublished Ph. D thesis, Indiana University, 1969. RWC

Bibliography: pp. 182-188.

SCHOENHALS, Lawrence Russell. Higher Education in the Free Methodist Church in the United States: 1860-1954. Unpublished Ph. D. dissertation, University of Washington, 1955. 501pp. FMHC RWC SPU

Bibiliography: pp. 454-464. Bibliography includes many citations on Free Methodist educational institutions over the years: Seattle Seminary, Seattle Pacific College, Evansville Seminary, Greenville College, Chili Seminary, Los Angeles Seminary, Campbell Free Methodist Seminary, McKinney Junior College, Spring Arbor Seminary, Central Academy, A. M. Chesbrough Seminary, Wessington Springs

Seminary. Some of these institutions are no longer in
existence or have changed their names.

EDUCATION - Handbooks
(No locations given)

AMERICAN Council on Education. American Universities and
Colleges. Washington, D. C., 1936-   .

COLLEGE Blue Book. Yonker-on-Hudson, New York, 1923-   .

COLLEGE Entrance Examination Board. The New York Times
Guide to Continuing Education in America. Frances
Coombs Thomson, ed. New York, New York: Quadrangle
Books, c1972. 816pp.

DIRECTORY of American Scholars: A Biographical Directory.
New York, New York: R. R. Bowker, 1942.

FINE, Benjamin. Barron's Profiles of American Colleges:
All the Facts You Need to Choose your College. Wood-
bury, New York: Barron's Educational Series, c1971.
882pp.

LOVEJOY, Clarence Earle. College Guide: A Complete Reference Book to American College and Universities.
Simon and Schuster, 1952-   .

NATIONAL Faculty Directory. Detroit, Michigan: Gale
Research, 1970-   .

REVELL'S Guide to Christian Colleges. Westwood, New Jersey:
F. H. Revell, 1965.

U. S. Office of Education. Education Directory: Higher
Education. Washington, D. C., 1961/62-   .

ESCHATOLOGY
(The Free Methodist Church takes no doctrinal stand on the
Millennium at this time.)

See also Aldersgate Doctrinal Studies in Sunday School
Curriculum section.

BALDWIN, Harmon Allen. The Coming Judgement: General and
at the End of Time. Chicago, Illinois: Free Methodist
Publishing House, 1927. 184pp. FMHC RWC SAC

HELSEL, E. Walter. "When is Jesus Coming Back?" Light
and Life, (November 9, 1976), pp. 6-7, 12. FMHC RWC
SAC SPU

SILVER, Jesse Forest. The Lord's Return. Seen in History
and in Scripture as Pre-Millennial and Imminent.
New York, New York: F. H. Revell, 1914. 311pp. FMHC
SAC

SIMS, Albert. Behold the Bridegroom Cometh: or Some Re-
markable and Incontrovertible Signs which Herald the
Near Approach of the Son of Man. Kingston, Ontario,
Canada. By author, 1900. FMHC

SIMS, Albert. Deepening Shadows and Coming Glories. Toronto, Ontario: By author, 1905. 256pp. FMHC SAC

EVANGELISM

DIETER, Melvin Easterday. Revivalism and Holiness. Unpublished Ph.D. dissertation, Temple University, 1973.
FMHC

FAIRBAIRN, Charles V. God's Plan for World Evangelism.
Winona Lake, Indiana: Light and Life Press, 1946.
117pp. FMHC SAC SPU

FAIRBAIRN, Charles V. A Primer on Evangelism. New

41

"Secret of True Revival." Winona Lake, Indiana: Light
and Life Press. c1947, 1955. FMHC SAC

FAIRBAIRN, Charles V. The Secret of True Revival. (Holiness Must Be Preached). Chicago, Illinois: Free Methodist Publishing House, 1929. 104pp. FMHC RWC

FAIRBAIRN, Charles V. A Symposium on Revivals and the
Present Day Need. Chicago, Illinois: Free Methodist
Publishing House, n.d. 176pp. SAC FMHC

HOGG, Wilson Thomas. Revivals and Revival Work. Buffalo,
New York: By author, c1890. 64pp. FMHC RWC SAC

JOHNSON, Carl E. How in the World? Winona Lake, Indiana:
Light and Life Press, c1969. 125pp. FMHC RWC

Bibliography: pp. 158-160. Last section by Marion Williamson Groesbeck.

KINGSLEY, Charles W. DO. Manifesto for Concerned Christ-
ian Community: Manual for Meaning in Mobilization of
Manpower. Winona Lake, Indiana: Light and Life Men
International, 1976. FMHC

KINGSLEY, Charles W. and George Delamarter. GO! Revolu-
tionary New Testament Christianity. Grand Rapids,
Michigan: Zondervan Publishing House, 1965. FMHC

ROBERTS, Benjamin Titus. Fishers of Men; or, Practical
Hints to Those Who Would Win Souls. Rochester, New
York: G. L. Roberts & Co., 1878. 272pp. FMHC RWC
SPU

ROBERTS, Benjamin Titus. Fishers of Men; or, Practical
Hints to Those Who Would Win Souls. Chicago, Illinois: W. B. Rose, 1918. 337pp. FMHC RWC SAC SPU

ROBERTS, Benjamin Titus. Fishers of Men; or, Practical

Hints to Those Who Would Win Souls. Winona Lake,
Indiana: Light and Life Press, 1948. 272pp. Reprint
of 1878 ed. FMHC

SMITH, Timothy Lawrence. Revivalism and Social Reform in
Mid-Nineteenth-Century America. New York, New York:
Abingdon Press, c1957. FMHC RWC

SNIDER, K. Lavern. Whose Ministry? Osaka, Japan: Japan
Free Methodist Mission, 1975. 150pp. FMHC

K. Lavern Snider is a Free Methodist Missionary to Japan.

WALTERS, Orville Selkirk. You Can Win Others: How to
Adventure in Sharing the Good News. Winona Lake,
Indiana: Light and Life Press, c1951, 1961. 82pp.
FMHC RWC

GLOSSALALIA

BASTIAN, Donald N. "Is There a Special Prayer Language?"
Light and Life, (February 24, 1976), pp. 6-7. FMHC
RWC   SAC   SPU

DUEWEL, Wesley L. Holy Spirit and Tongues. Winona Lake,
Indiana: Light and Life Press, 1974. FMHC

Duewel deals with the modern-day aspects of speaking in
tongues.

KNOX, Lloyd H. Key Biblical Perspectives on Tongues.
Winona Lake, Indiana: Light and Life, 1974. FMHC

SHELHAMER, Ernest E. Five Reasons Why I Do Not Seek the
Gift of Tongues. 4th ed. "The Repairer", n.d. RWC

AN ACT to Incorporate the Free Methodist Church in Canada. Ottawa, Canada: Queen's Printer and Controller of Stationery, 1959. 17pp. FMHC

ASIA Fellowship Conference, Osaka, 1960. Asia Fellowship Conference, April 19-28 (1960) Osaka, Japan; a Compilation of Reports, Documents, Interpretation. Frank J. Kline, ed. Winona Lake, Indiana: Continuing Committee of the Free Methodist World Fellowship, North American Division (1960). 112pp. FMHC

BOWEN, Elias. History of the Origin of the Free Methodist Church. Rochester, New York: B. T. Roberts, 1871. 350pp. FMHC RWC SAC SPU

"Sketch of the life of the author," by B. T. Roberts, pp. iii-viii. Bowen details the climate that produced the Free Methodist Church - secret societies, war, unjustified expulsions, persecutions, and the "worldliness" of the Methodists.

BRATT, J. "Who Are the Free Methodists?" Banner, (September 21, 1973), p. 14. FMHC RWC SAC SPU

BURLINGHAM, C. D. An Outline History of the Genesee Conference Difficulties. n.p., 1860. 61pp. FMHC

CHESBROUGH, Samuel K. J. Defense of Rev. B. T. Roberts, A.M. Before the Genesee Conference of the Methodist Episcopal Church at Perry, New York, October 13-21, 1858. Buffalo, New York: Clapp, Matthews and Company's Steam Printing House, 1858. FMHC

Taken from notes and testimony written during the trial.

DEMARAY, Donald E. "Rich, Our Wesley Heritage!" Light and Life. (April 11, 1972), p. 16. FMHC RWC SAC SPU

FAIRBAIRN, C. V. Journals. 1939-1961. Unpublished manu-
script.No. 19, Accession List. Free Methodist Historical Center.

1929-1961 were the years of Fairbairn's Bishopric.

FEDERAL Writers' Project. New York (State). Rochester and
Monroe County...Rochester, New York: Scranton's, c1937.
460pp. RWC

FREE METHODIST Church. Eighty Years Historical Sketch WMS,
1894-1974. Winona Lake, Indiana: Woman's Missionary
Society, 1974. 50pp. FMHC

GADDIS, Vincent H. The Story of Winona Lake: A Memory and
a Vision, A Remarkable Story of the World's Largest
Bible Conference, Its Personalities and Its Future.
Berne, Indiana: Berne Witness, 1949. 107pp. RWC FMHC

HART, Edward Payson. Reminiscences of Early Free Methodism. Chicago, Illinois: Free Methodist Publishing
House, 1913. 259pp. FMHC RWC SAC SPU

Edward P. Hart was the 2nd Free Methodist Bishop.

HASLAM, Robert B. "Free...Heritage of Faith and Life."
Light and Life, (July 10, 1973), p. 3. FMHC RWC SAC
SPU

HASLAM, Robert B. "What Does the 'Free' in Free Methodism
Mean?" Light and Life, (January 20, 1976), pp. 10-11.
FMHC RWC SAC SPU

HITT, Russell T. Story of the Light and Life Hour.
Winona Lake, Indiana: Forward Movement of the Free
Methodist Church, n.d. 10pp. FMHC

Reprint from Christian Life magazine.

✓ HOGUE, Wilson Thomas. History of the Free Methodist Church of North America. Chicago, Illinois: Free Methodist Publishing House, 1915. 2v. FMHC RWC SAC SPU

Standard history of Free Methodism until the publication of Leslie R. Marston's From Age to Age a Living Witness.

HOGUE, Wilson Thomas. Retrospect and Prospect. A Semi-Centennial Sermon (50 Years). Chicago, Illinois: Free Methodist Publishing House, 1911. FMHC

Preached before the General Conference, June 18, 1911.

ⅩHOWLAND, Carl L. The Story of Our Church: Free Methodism, Some Facts and Some Reasons. Winona Lake, Indiana: Free Methodist Publishing House, 1939. 156pp. FMHC RWC SAC SPU

KENDALL, W. C. Dairy, 1857. Unpublished Manuscript. No. 61, Documentary Record. Free Methodist Historical Center.

KYSOR, Kenneth. Sweeter as the Years Go By: A History of Roberts Memorial (Church). Cattaraugus, New York: By author, c1976. 20pp. RWC FMHC

LAKE, Charles T. Our Goodly Heritage; a History of the Gerry Homes. Gerry, New York: Heritage Village, 1971. 46pp. RWC FMHC

Gerry Homes is one of the Free Methodist benevolent institutions.

Ⅹ MACGEARY, John Samuel. The Free Methodist Church: A Brief Outline History of Its Origin and Development. Chicago, Illinois: W. B. Rose, 1908. 224pp. FMHC RWC SAC

MANN, William Edward. Sect, Cult and Church in Alberta. Toronto, University of Toronto Press, 1955. 166pp.

MANUAL on Pentecost Bands. Unpublished manuscript.
No. 43/44, Documentary Record. Free Methodist Historical Center, 1885.

Handwritten. This volume also includes the record book of
the early Parma-Albion, Michigan circuit.

MARSTON, Leslie R. "The American Camp Meetings – Then and
Now." Light and Life, (June 22, 1976), p. 10. FMHC
RWC SAC SPU

✗ MARSTON, Leslie Ray. From Age to Age a Living Witness:
A Historical Interpretation of Free Methodism's First
Century. Winona Lake, Indiana: Light and Life Press,
1960. 608pp. FMHC RWC SAC SPU
ın this volume the aim of
"Interprets Methodism from the time of John Wesley
through Free Methodism's first century, featuring doctrinal
and practical trends." L. R. Marston's work is involved of
diverse. He utilizes a of he many primary sources.

METHODIST Episcopal Church. Genesee Annual Conference.
Minutes. LeRoy, New York, September 10, 1851. Buffalo,
New York: Steam Press of G. Reese and Co., 1851. FMHC

MINUTES of the Genesee Annual Conference of the Methodist
Episcopal Church held at LeRoy, New York, September 10th,
1851. Buffalo, New York: Steam Press of G. Reese and
Co., 1851. FMHC

MOORE, Carl C. Chili Chapters: A Condensation of Chili's
History Based Primarily on Town Records. A Sesquincen-
tennial Publication, c1972. 64pp. FMHC RWC

ORTON, M. Diary, 1858. No. 28, Accession List. Free
Methodist Historical Center.

OUR CHURCH in this Age. Pastoral Address. Winona Lake,
Indiana: Free Methodist Publishing House, 1939. FMHC

PARRY, Albert W. St. Charles Camp Meeting of 1885. n.p., n.d. FMHC

POSTE, Donald E. "Centenary of Free Methodism, 1860-1960." Historical Wyoming, (April, 1960), pp. 65-93. FMHC

PROJECTING Our Heritage. Papers and Messages delivered at the Centennial Convention of the National Holiness Association, Cleveland, Ohio, April 16-19, 1968. Myron F. Boyd and Merne A. Harris, comp. Kansas City, Missouri: Beacon Hill Press, 1969. FMHC

REINHARD, James Arnold. Personal and Sociological Factors in the Formation of the Free Methodist Church, 1852-1869. Unpublished Ph.D. dissertation, University of Iowa, 1971. 254pp. FMHC

ROBERTS, Benjamin Titus. Why Another Sect; Containing a Review of Articles by Bishop Simpson and others on the Free Methodist Church. Rochester, New York: "The Earnest Christian" Publishing House, 1879. 321pp. FMHC   RWC   SAC   SPU

SELLEW, Walter. Four Travel Journals by Bishop Sellew. Unpublished manuscript. No. 77, Documentary Record. Free Methodist Historical Center.

SIGSWORTH, John Wilkins. The Battle Was the Lord's. A History of the Free Methodist Church in Canada. Oshawa, Ontario: Sage Publishers, 1960. FMHC   SAC   SPU

SIMS, Albert, ed. Free Methodism in Canada. Consisting of the Origin and Growth of Free Methodism in Canada; A Report of the Proceedings of the First Canadian Free Methodism Convention, held at Sarnia, October 13-18, 1920; and a Statement as to the Doctrines, Usages and Church Government of the Free Methodist People. Toronto, Ontario: By author, n.d.   FMHC   RWC

SMITH, David Paul. The Growth and Development of the Interracial Movement within the Free Methodist Church of North America. Unpublished research paper, Asbury Theological Seminary, Wilmore, Kentucky, 195?. FMHC

TAYLOR, Jesse Paul. Goodly Heritage. Winona Lake, Indiana: Light and Life Press, 1960. 138pp. FMHC RWC SAC

TENNEY, Mary Alice. "Free!" Free Methodist, (December, 1967), p. 12. FMHC RWC SAC SPU

B. T. Roberts had a deep social concern involving free pews and anti-slavery sentiment.

TERRILL, Joseph Goodwin. The St. Charles' Camp-Meeting, Embodying Its History and Several Sermons by Leading Ministers, with some Practical Suggestions concerning Camp Meeting Management. Chicago, Illinois: T. B. Arnold, 1883. FMHC RWC SAC

ZAHNISER, Arthur. "Perspective: Our Small Group Heritage." Light and Life, (June 5, 1973), p. 14. FMHC RWC SAC SPU

HISTORY - General Works with references to Free Methodism. (No locations given but all available at FMHC)

AHLSTROM, Sidney E. A Religious History of the American People. New Haven, Connecticut, 1972.

ALLEN, Ray. A Century of the Genesee Annual Conference of the Methodist Episcopal Church, 1810-1910. Rochester, New York: By author, 1911.

References to Free Methodism, pp. 9-10.

AMERICAN Church of the Protestant Heritage. Vergilius Ferm, ed. New York, New York: Philosophical Library, 1953. 481pp.

BUCKLEY, James Monroe. A History of Methodists in the United States. New York, New York: The Christian Literature Co., 1896. 714pp.

A Methodist perspective is given to the trial and expulsion of B. T. Roberts which was the event that led to the formation of the Free Methodist Church. Buckley also lists the extensive educational institutions founded by the Free Methodists.

FM - pp. 503, 614, 615.

BUCKLEY, James Monroe. A History of Methodism in the United States. New York, New York: Harper and Bros., 1898. 2v.

FM - various references.

BRAUER, Jerold C. The Westminster Dictionary of Church History. Philadelphia, Pennsylvania: Westminster Press, 1971.

Free Methodism is placed in perspective within the Methodist movement.

FM - p. 546.

CAMERON, Richard M. Methodism and Society. New York, New York: Abingdon Press, 1961.

FM v. 1, pp. 87, 265.

CLARK, Elmer T. An Album of Methodism History. New York: Abingdon-Cokesbury Press, 1952.

FM - p. 308. Clark gives a concise summary of the origins of the Free Methodist Church.

CLARK, Elmer T. The Small Sects in America. Nashville, Tennessee: Cokesbury Press, 1937.

FM - pp. 85, 86, 91, 99.

CLARK, Elmer T. The Small Sects in America. New York, New York: Abingdon-Cokesbury Press, 1949.

FM - pp. 63-64.

⤬ CONABLE, F. W. History of the Genesee Annual Conference
    of the Methodist Episcopal Church from Its Organization
    by Bishops Asbury and McKendree, in 1810, to the year
    1884: Embracing the more important proceedings on
    every session, with notes of the times, and notices of
    the educational and other enterprises of the church;
    of the divisions of the conference, and of the arrange-
    ment of the itinerant work from year to year; pioneer
    experiences, remarkable revivals and conversions, bio-
    graphical sketches, reminiscences, incidents, anecdotes,
    etc. New York, New York: Phillips and Hunt, 1885.
    2nd ed.

FM - various references. For another point of view on
Free Methodist beginnings, consult B. T. Roberts', Why
Another Sect?

CURTISS, George, ed. Manual of Methodist Episcopal Church
    History showing the Evolution of Methodism in the United
    States of America for the use of Students and General
    Readers. New York, New York: Hunt and Eaton, c1892,
    1893.

FM - p. 228.

⤬ CYCLOPAEDIA of Methodism; embracing sketches of its rise,
    progress and present condition, with biographical no-
    tices and numerous illustrations. Matthew Simpson, ed.
    Philadelphia, Pennsylvania: Everts and Stewart, c1876,
    1878.

FM - pp. 379-380.

DANIELS, W. H. The Illustrated History of Methodism in
    Great Britain and America from the Days of the Wesleys
    to the Present Time. New York, New York: Phillips
    and Hunt, c1879, 1880.

FM - p. 703.

DAYTON, Donald W. Discovering an Evangelical Heritage.
   New York, New York: Harper and Row, 1976.   FMHC

FM - pp. 92-102.

FAULKNER, John Alfred. The Methodists: The Story of the
   Churches. New York, New York: Baker and Taylor Co.,
   1903.

FM - p. 173.

FERGUSON, Charles W. Organizing to Beat the Devil: Methodists and the Making of America. Garden City, New
   York: Doubleday, 1971.

FM - pp. 277-278.

GARBER, Paul Neff. The Methodists Are One People. Nashville, Tennessee: Cokesbury Press, 1939.

FM - pp. 32-33, 72, 138.

HISTORY of American Methodism. New York, New York: Abingdon Press, 1964. 3v.

FM - v. III, pp. 589, 592.

HUDSON, Winthrop Still. Religion in America. New York,
   New York: Scribner, 1965.

HURST, John Fletcher. American Methodism. New York, New
   York: Eaton and Mains, c1902, 1903. 3 v.

FM - pp. 1088-1115.

HYDE, Ammi Bradford. The Story of Methodism: Tracing the
   Rise and Progress of that Wonderful Religious Movement,
   which, like the gulf stream, has given warmth to wide
   waters and verdure to many lands; and giving an account
   of its various influences and institutions of today.

New York, New York: M. W. Hazen, c1887, 1888.

FM - pp. 317-325.

JONES, Charles Edwin. Perfectionist Persuasion: The
Holiness Movement and American Methodism, 1867-1936.
Metuchen, New Jersey: Scarecrow Press, 1974. 242pp.

Includes bibliographies.

KELLEY, Dean M. Why Conservative Churches Are Growing:
A Study in Sociology of Religion. New York, New York:
Harper and Row, 1972.

FM - p. 25.

LATOURETTE, Kenneth Scott. A History of the Expansion
of Christianity. Zondervan, c1944, 1970.

FM - v. 4, p. 444; v. 5, pp. 362, 387, 402; v. 6, pp.
178, 344.

LEE, James W., Naphtali Luccock and James Main Dixon.
The Illustrated History of Methodism: The Story of the
Origin and Progress of the Methodist Church, from its
Foundation by John Wesley to the present day. St.
Louis, Missouri: The Methodist Magazine, 1900.

FM - pp. 559-560.

LEETE, Frederick DeLand. Methodist Bishops: Personal
Notes and Bibliography with Quotations from Unpublished
Writings and Reminiscences. Nashville, Tennessee:
Parthenon Press, 1948.

FM - various references.

MCLEISTER, Ira Ford. History of the Wesleyan Methodist
Church of America. Syracuse, New York: Wesleyan Methodist Publishing Association, 1934.

MASER, F. E., ed. "Church Trial of Early Methodists."
  Methodist History, (June, 1971), pp. 57-61.

MERRILL, Arch. Stagecoach Towns. Rochester, New York:
  Gannett, 1947. 186pp.

MILNER, Vincent L. Religious Denominations of the World:
  Comprising a General View of the Origin, History, and
  Condition of the Various Sects of Christians, the Jews,
  and Mahometans, as well as the Pagan Forms of Religion
  Existing in the Different Countries of the Earth;
  with Sketches of the Founders of various Religious
  Sects from the Best Authorities. Philadelphia, Penn-
  sylvania: Bradley, Garretson, 1871. 622pp.

FM - pp. 606-608.

NORWOOD, John Nelson. The Schism in the Methodist Episcopal Church, 1844: A Study of Slavery and Ecclesiastical Politics. Alfred, New York: Alfred University,
  The Alfred Press, 1923.

FM - p. 225.

NORWOOD, Frederick A. The Story of American Methodism:
  History of the United Methodist and Their Relations.
  Nashville, Tennessee: Abingdon Press, 1974.

FM - pp. 294-297, 375-376.

ORR, J. Edwin. The Light of the Nations: Evangelical
  Renewal and Advance in the Nineteenth Century. Grand
  Rapids, Michigan: W. B. Eerdmans, 1965.

FM - p. 208.

RELIGION in American Life. James Ward Smith and A. Le-
  land Jamison, ed's. Princeton, New Jersey: Princeton
  University Press, 1961.

SELLEW, Walter A. Obligations of Civilization to Christ-

ianity or The Influence of Christianity upon Civilization. Chicago, Illinois: Light and Life Press, 1928.

Walter Sellew was the 5th Free Methodist Bishop.

SIMPSON, Matthew. A Hundred Years of Methodism. New York,
New York: Nelson and Phillips, c1876, 1879.

FM - pp. 323-324.

SMITH, Timothy L. Called Unto Holiness: The Story of the
Nazarenes, the Formative Years. Kansas City, Missouri:
Nazarene Publishing House, c1962, 1963.

FM - various references.

SMITH, Timothy L. Revivalism and Social Reform in Mid-
Nineteenth-Century America. New York, New York: Abingdon Press, 1957.

FM - various references.

SNYDER, Howard Albert. Unity and the Holiness Churches.
A Study of Moves Toward Unity Among Selected American
Protestant Denominations affiliated with the National
Holiness Association. Unpublished M.A. thesis, Asbury
Theological Seminary, 1966.

STEVENS, Abel. History of the Methodist Episcopal Church
in the United States of America. New York, New York,
1964. 2v.

SWEET, William Warren. Methodism in American History.
Nashville, Tennessee: Abingdon Press, c1954, 1961.

FM - pp. 326, 341.

SYNAN, Vinson. The Holiness-Pentecostal Movement in the
United States. Grand Rapids, Michigan: W. B. Eerdmans Publishing Co., 1971.

FM - pp. 75, 145.

TOWNSEND, W. J., H. B. Workman, and George Eayrs, ed's.
   A New History of Methodism. London: Hodder and Stough-
   ton, 1909. 2v.

FM - various references.

HISTORY - Handbooks & Encyclopedias
(No locations given)

CORPUS Dictionary of Western Churches. T. C. O'Brien, ed.
   Washington, D. C: Corpus Publications, 1970.

FM - p. 335. Gives brief summary of history, doctrinal
stands, missionary programs and affiliations of Western
Churches.

CYCLOPEDIA of Biblical, Theological and Ecclesiastical
   Literature. John McClintock and James Strong, ed's.
   New York, New York: Harper and Bros., 1876.

FM - v. 6, pp. 158-159, 187-189.

ECUMENICAL Directory of Retreat and Conference Centers.
   Denver, Colorado: Jarrow Press, n.d.

ENCYCLOPEDIA Britannica. 11th ed. Cambridge, England:
   University Press.

FM - v. XVIII, p. 297.

ENCYCLOPEDIA of Associations. Detroit, Michigan: Gale
   Research Co., 1956-   .

ENCYCLOPEDIA of World Methodism. Nolan B. Harmon, ed.
   World Methodist Council and The Commission on Archives
   and History of The United Methodist Church. 2v.

FM - pp. 876-880.

GAUSTED, Edwin Scott. Historical Atlas of Religion in
America. New York, New York: Harper and Row, 1912.

FM - p. 125.

HANDBOOK of Denominations in the United States. Frank S.
Mead, ed. 6th ed. Nashville, Tennessee: Abingdon
Press, 1975.

FM - pp. 194-195. Includes history, doctrine, organization of each denomination.

NEW Catholic Encyclopedia. New York, New York: McGraw-
Hill, 1967.

PICTORIAL HISTORY of Protestantism: A Panoramic View of
Western Europe and the United States. Vergilius Ferm,
ed. New York, New York: Philosophical Library, 1957.

FM - pp. 300-301. Includes pictures of B. T. Roberts, the
Albion Church, the first building of Roberts Wesleyan College and the Free Methodist World Headquarters.

RELIGIOUS Bodies: 1936. Washington, D.C: U. S. Department of Commerce, 1941.

FM - v. 1, pp. 407, 441; v. 2, pt. 2, p. 1153. Very in-
formative compilation of statistics on church membership
and expenditures as well as brief comments on the history,
doctrines, and organization of the Free Methodist Church.

STATE of the Churches in the United States of America -
1973, As Shown in their own Official Yearbooks. Sun
City, Arizona: Ecumenism Research Agency, 1973.

FM - p. 18.

WORLD BOOK Encyclopedia. Field Enterprises, 1976.

FM - v. 7, p. 426.

WORLD Christian Handbook. Wakelin H. Coxill and Sir Kenneth Grubb, ed's. Nashville, Tennessee: Abingdon Press, 1967.

Includes general articles on religious trends as well as a directory of churches with addresses for church and mission headquarters.

YEARBOOK of American and Canadian Churches, 1975. Constant H. Jacquet, ed. Nashville, Tennessee: Abingdon Press, 1967.

FM - p. 60. The yearbook updates organizational information on the officers and periodicals of each denomination.

HOLINESS MOVEMENT CHURCH. (merged with the Free Methodist Church in 1958)

A BRIEF History of Holiness Movement Missions, 1899-1959. Young People's Missionary Society, n.d. FMHC

On missions of the Holiness Movement in Egypt and Hong Kong.

HOLINESS Movement Church. Catechism. n.p. 1935, 1943. FMHC

HORNER, R. C. Bible Doctrines. Ottawa, Canada: Holiness Movement Publishing House, 1908, FMHC

HORNER, R. C. Bible Doctrines, Volume II. Ottawa, Canada: Holiness Movement Publishing House, 1909. FMHC

HORNER, R. C. The Doctrine and Discipline of the Holiness Movement (or Church) Ottawa, Canada: By author, 1900- ?. FMHC

HORNER, Ralph C. From the Altar to the Upper Room in Four Parts. Toronto, Ontario, Canada: William Briggs, c1891.   FMHC

This book led to the founding of the Holiness Movement
Church.

HOLINESS MOVEMENT CHURCH. - Periodicals.

THE CANADIAN Methodist and Holiness Era.   Toronto, Ontario.
    1-?, 189?-1958.   FMHC

This periodical merged in 1959 with the Free Methodist.

THE MAGAZINE of the Holiness Movement Church.   1-?, 1909-?
    FMHC

This periodical ran concurrent to The Canadian Methodist
and Holiness Era for a short time and then ended.

HOMILETICS AND THE MINISTRY

COOK, Arnold Willis.   An Analysis of the Responsibilities
    and Training of Selected Ministers in Church Business
    Administration.   Unpublished M. A. thesis, East Tennes-
    see State University, 1970.   FMHC

DEMARAY, Donald E.   An Introduction to Homiletics.   Grand
    Rapids, Michigan: Baker Book House, 1974.   156pp.
    FMHC   RWC

DEMARAY, Donald E.   Minister's Ministries.   Winona Lake,
    Indiana: Light and Life Press, 1974.   36pp.   FMHC   RWC

DEMARAY, Donald E.   Preacher Aflame! Grand Rapids, Michi-
    gan: Baker Book House, 1972.   87pp.   FMHC   RWC

DEMARAY, Donald E.   Pulpit Giants: What Made Them Great.
    Chicago, Illinois: Moody Press, 1973.   174pp.   FMHC
    RWC

DEMARAY, Donald E. A Pulpit Manual. Winona Lake, Indiana: Light and Life Press, 1959. 64pp. FMHC

"FOCUS on Pastoral Ministry." Light and Life, (March 23, 1976), pp. 10-11. FMHC SPU

FREE METHODIST Minister. Lloyd H. Knox, ed., comp. Winona Lake, Indiana: Light and Life Press, 1976. 90pp. FMHC

Manual for Free Methodist ministers giving the rituals for Baptism, Communion, Marriage, Burial, etc. from the Free Methodist Discipline as well as Scriptures for various special services.

GALBREATH, Marvin L. Twenty Centuries of Christianity. Winona Lake, Indiana: Light and Life Press, 1970. 80pp. FMHC

HOGG, Wilson Thomas. A Hand-Book of Homiletics and Pastoral Theology. 3rd. ed. Chicago, Illinois: Free Methodist Publishing House, c1886, 1895. FMHC

HOGUE, Wilson Thomas. A Hand-Book of Homiletics and Pastoral Theology. Chicago, Illinois: T. B. Arnold, 1887. FMHC RWC

HOGUE, Wilson Thomas. Handbook of Homiletics and Pastoral Theology. 5th ed. Chicago, Illinois: Free Methodist Publishing House, c1886, 1906. 454pp. FMHC SAC

HOGUE, Wilson Thomas. A Hand-Book of Homiletics and Pastoral Theology. 2nd ed. Chicago, Illinois: Free Methodist Publishing House, 1914. FMHC

HOGUE, Wilson Thomas. A Handbook of Homiletics and Pastoral Theology. Chicago, Illinois: Free Methodist Publishing House, 1924. 454pp. RWC

HOGUE, Wilson Thomas. A Handbook of Homiletics and Pastoral Theology. 11th ed. Winona Lake, Indiana: Free
Methodist Publishing House, 1940. 454pp. RWC

MILLER, Donald G. The Way to Biblical Preaching. New
York, Abingdon Press, 1957. FMHC

NORTHRUP, Lyle W. Ancient Mirrors for Modern Churches: A
Study of the Seven Churches of the Book of Revelation
regulating them to the Church in Modern Society. Winona
Lake, Indiana: Light and Life Press, 1973. 60pp. FMHC

ROBERTS, Benjamin Titus. Letters Dealing with Pastoral
Problems. Unpublished manuscript. No. 83, Documentary
Record. Free Methodist Historical Center.

SHELHAMER, Ernest Ellsworth. Heart Searching Talks to
Ministers. Louisville, Kentucky, 1914. 272pp. FMHC
RWC SAC

TURNBULL, Ralph G. A History of Preaching. Grand Rapids,
Michigan: Baker Book House, 1974. 586pp. FMHC

Includes reference to Free Methodist preacher, L. R. Marston.

HYMNALS AND SONGBOOKS

CAMP Meeting Special. A Selection of Songs Specially Designed for Use in Camp Mee ings and Other Evangelistic
Campaigns. Winona Lake, Indiana: Light and Life Press,
n.d. FMHC

CHOICE Light and Life Songs. A Collection of the Best
Loved Gospel Songs and Choruses, both Old and New...
for Sunday School, Young People's Meeting, Evangelistic Service and Children's Service. LeRoy M. Lowell,
et. al., comp. Winona Lake, Indiana: Light and Life
Press, 1950. FMHC

CHOICE HYMNS. A Collection of Hymns from the Free Methodist Hymnal especially adapted for Revival Services. William Pearce, et. al., comp. Winona Lake, Indiana: Free Methodist Publishing House, 1942. FMHC

FREE METHODIST Church. General Conference Songbook (One Way to a Whole World). Winona Lake, Indiana: Light and Life Press, 1974. FMHC SPU

FREE METHODIST Church. Joyfully Sing: A Hymnal for Children. Joy Latham, comp. Kansas City, Missouri: Lillenas Publishing Co., 1968. FMHC

Published by both the Free Methodist Church and the Wesleyan Church.

GOSPEL Truths in Song; Adapted especially to Sunday School, Social Worship, Camp Meetings and Revival Services. William Backus Olmstead, comp. Chicago, Illinois: W. B. Rose, 1915. FMHC

INSPIRATIONAL Songs for the Sunday School, Social Worship, Missionary and Evangelistic Work. Newton W. Fink, Joseph B. Lutz, W. B. Rose, comp. Chicago, Illinois: Light and Life Press, 1924. FMHC RWC

LIGHT and Life Songs...Adapted especially to Sunday Schools, Prayer Meetings, and other Social Services. William B. Olmstead and Thoro Harris, ed's. Chicago, Illinois: W. B. Rose, 1904. FMHC RWC

LIGHT and Life Songs. Number Two. Adapted especially to Sunday Schools, Social Worship, Camp Meetings, and Revival Services. William B. Olmstead and Thoro Harris ed's. Chicago, Illinois: W. B. Rose, 1914. FMHC

LIGHT and Life Songs. Number Three. For Sunday Schools, Social Worship, Camp Meetings, and Revival Services. William B. Olmstead, ed. Chicago, Illinois: 1918. FMHC

LIGHT and Life Songs. Number Four. For the Sunday School,
     Social Worship, Missionary and Evangelistic Work. Will-
     iam B. Olmstead and Mr. and Mrs. Newton W. Fink, comp.
     and ed. Chicago, Illinois: Light and Life Press, 1928.
     FMHC

PHILLIPS, Philip. et. al. Metrical Tune Book. Chicago,
     Illinois: T. B. Arnold, 1890. 230pp. FMHC SPU

Includes numbers and hymns from the Free Methodist Hymn
Book with each tune.

PHILLIPS, Philip. et. al. Metrical Tune Book. rev. ed.
     Chicago, Illinois: T. B. Arnold, 1898. 309pp. SPU

MISSIONARY Hymns and Responsive Scripture Readings: For use
     in Missionary Meetings. Wilson Thomas Hogue, comp.
     Chicago, Illinois: Woman's Foreign Missionary Society
     of the Free Methodist Church, c1907, 1928. FMHC RWC

SPIRITUAL Songs and Hymns for Pilgrims. B. T. Roberts,
     comp. Rochester, New York: B. T. Roberts, 1868.
     FMHC RWC

VOICES of Praise. Prepared with especial Reference to the
     Needs of the Sunday School. It will also be found suit-
     able for the prayer meeting and other Religious Gath-
     erings. William B. Olmstead, et. al., comp. Chicago,
     Illinois: W. B. Rose, 1909?. FMHC

WORSHIP in Song. An All Purpose Song Book for use in the
     church but especially adapted for use in the Sunday
     School, Missionary, Young People's and Evangelistic
     Services. William Pearce, et. al., comp. Chicago,
     Illinois: Light and Life Press, 1935. FMHC RWC SPU

HYMNS - History and Criticism

BASTIAN, Donald. "Bishop's Column: Wesley tells how to

sing." Light and Life, (October 7, 1975), p. 2. FMHC
RWC   SAC   SPU

HOGUE, Wilson Thomas. Hymns that are Immortal, with some
    account of their Authorship, Origin, History, and In-
    fluence. 2nd ed. Chicago, Illinois: S.K.J. Chesbrough,
    c1906. 325pp.   FMHC   RWC   SAC

INSTRUMENTAL Music in Publish Worship. The Position Held
    by the Free Methodist Church. E. A. Andrews, ed. Chi-
    cago, Illinois: Free Methodist Publishing House, 1927.
    44pp.   FMHC   RWC   SPU

This statement was ordered published by its 17th General
Conference and supported the original position of the Free
Methodist Church that no instrumental music should be used.
This has since been changed.

KAUFMANN, U. Milo. "The Hymns as a First-Person Report."
    Light and Life, (November 9, 1971), p. 9.   FMHC   RWC
    SAC   SPU

MACGEARY, John S. Some Objections to the Use of Instru-
    mental Music in Religious Worship Services Considered.
    Farnham Printing Co., n.d.   RWC

MARSTON, Leslie R. and Wilson T. Hogue. The Living Hymns
    of Charles Wesley. Winona Lake, Indiana: Light and
    Life Press, 1957. 64pp.   FMHC   RWC   SAC   SPU

Includes The Singing Saint, selections from Hymns That Are
Immortal and selections from Charles Wesley's Hymn Poems.

SCHOENHALS, Lawrence R. "Hymnody in a Disposable Society."
    Light and Life, (January 25, 1972), p. 5.   FMHC   RWC
    SAC   SPU

SCHOENHALS, Lawrence R. "Singing with the Understanding
    Also." The Christian Minister, (Spring, 1949), p. 25.
    FMHC

SCHOENHALS, Lawrence R. "Our New Hymnal." Light and Life,
(October 7, 1975), pp. 6-7. FMHC RWC SAC SPU

TROMBLE, William W. "Finally – New Hymnal!" Light and
Life, (October 12, 1976), p. 10. FMHC RWC SAC SPU

TROMBLE, William W. "Music Is the Key." Light and Life,
(October 7, 1975), p. 5. FMHC RWC SAC SPU

HYMNS - Official Free Methodist Hymnals

FREE METHODIST Church. Free Methodist Hymnal. Chicago,
Illinois: Free Methodist Publishing House, c1910.
498pp. FMHC RWC SAC SPU

FREE METHODIST Church. Free Methodist Hymnal, published
by authority of the Free Methodist Church of North
America. Chicago, Illinois: Free Methodist Publishing
House, 1915. 497pp. FMHC SPU

FREE METHODIST Church. The Hymn Book of the Free Methodist Church. Rochester, New York: B. T. Roberts, 1883.
582pp. FMHC RWC SPU

FREE METHODIST Church. The Hymn Book of the Free Methodist
Church. Rochester, New York: B. T. Roberts, 1885.
591pp. FMHC SPU

FREE METHODIST Church. The Hymn Book of the Free Methodist
Church. Rochester, New York: B. T. Roberts, 1898.
FMHC RWC

FREE METHODIST Church. The Hymn Book of the Free Methodist
Church. Rochester, New York: B. T. Roberts, 1906.
FMHC RWC

FREE METHODIST Church. Hymns of Faith and Life. Lawrence

R. Schoenhals, ed. Winona Lake, Indiana: Light and
Life Press and the Wesley Press, c1976. 576pp. FMHC
SPU

FREE METHODIST Church. Hymns of the Living Faith. LeRoy
M. Lowell, ed. Winona Lake, Indiana: Light and Life
Press, 1951. FMHC RWC SAC SPU

MERGERS

"FREE Methodist and Wesleyan Boards agree, but Merger given
more time." Light and Life, (June 18, 1974), pp. 6-7.
FMHC SPU

HUFFMAN, J. "Free Methodist Vitality." Christian Century,
(July 18, 1969), p. 37. SPU

Discussion on merger between Wesleyans and Free Methodists.

JOINT Commission of the Free Methodist and Holiness Movement Church. Report of the Committee on Union being a
Summary of the Proceedings of the Joint Committee which
met in Kingston, Ontario, Canada. October 7-8, 1958.
Winona Lake, Indiana: Free Methodist Publishing House,
1958.

"In which Delegates from the Holiness Movement Church in
Canada met with a Free Methodist Delegation to Discuss
and Arrange for Union with the Latter. The completed merger arrangements as Presented to and Adapted by the Board
of Administration of the Free Methodist Church in Historic
Session." Published by order of the Joint Committee on
Union. FMHC

JOINT Commission of the Free Methodist and Wesleyan Methodist Churches. Proposed discipline for the United Wesleyan Methodist Church, n. p., 1955. 122pp. FMHC

JOINT Commission of the Free Methodist and Wesleyan Methodist Churches. Tentative Report, n. p., 1951. FMHC

"REPORT on Merger." _Light and Life_, (September 7, 1976),
    pp. 9, 12.

On merger between the Free Methodist Church and the Wesleyan Church.

SNYDER, H.A. "Wesleyan Wishing Well." _Christianity
    Today_, (May 10, 1976), pp. 50-51.   FMHC   SPU

Expresses optimism for the eventual merger of the Wesleyan
and Free Methodist denominations.

"WINONA '74 Keyword: Action!" _Light and Life_, (July 23,
    1974), pp. 3-8.

On merger between the Free Methodist Church and the Wesleyan church.

MISSION FIELDS - Biography, History (Includes Stories)
(Divided by geographical area)

AFRICA

ALLEN, F. Grace. Diary, 1889-1897, Africa. Unpublished
    manuscript. No. 62, Documentary Record. Free Methodist
    Historical Center.

COX, Betty Ellen. Mwene of the Congo. Winona Lake, Indi-
    ana: Light and Life Press, 1963.   FMHC

DEMILLE, Lela. Black Gold: A Story of Mozambique and
    Transvaal. Winona Lake, Indiana: Light and Life
    Press, 1966.   FMHC

JMS/CYC Series.

EMBREE, Esther. Chikombedzi. Winona Lake, Indiana:
    Light and Life Press, 1973.   FMHC

GHORMLEY, Newton Baxter. Land of the Heart of Livingstone. Chicago, Illinois: Free Methodist Publishing House, 1920. FMHC

HALEY, John Wesley. But Thy Right Hand. Winona Lake, Indiana: Woman's Missionary Society of the Free Methodist Church, 1949. 168pp. FMHC   RWC   SPU

HALEY, John Wesley. Life in Mozambique and South Africa. Free Methodist Publishing House, c1926. 174pp. FMHC RWC   SAC

HAVILAND, Emma Hillman. Under the Southern Cross, or a Woman's Life World for Africa. Cincinnati, Ohio: God's Bible School and Revivalist, 1928. 461pp. SPU

HENDICKSON, Ford. The Livingstone of the Orinoco. Wauseon, Ohio, 1942.

HOGUE, Emma L. Africa: A Mission Study for Juniors. 4th ed. Chicago, Illinois: Woman's Foreign Missionary Society of the Free Methodist Church, 1920. FMHC

HOGUE, Wilson Thomas. G. Harry Agnew: A Pioneer Missionary. Chicago, Illinois: Free Methodist Publishing House, 1905. 317pp. FMHC   RWC   SAC

HOUSER, Gwen and Jean Johnson. Boadi and Tembi of Africa's Grasslands. Winona Lake, Indiana: Light and Life Press, 1969. FMHC

On Rhodesia and South Africa. JMS/CYC Series.

HOUSER, Tillman. Church Growth in South Rhodesia, 1963. Unpublished manuscript. Free Methodist Historical Center.

KELLEY, Walter W. Memoirs of Mrs. Augusta Tullis Kelley: Her Experience, Labors as Evangelist and Missionary to

Africa, with Extracts from her Writings. Chicago, Illinois: T. B. Arnold, 1889. FMHC RWC

MACY, Victor W. A History of the Free Methodist Mission in Portugese East Africa. Unpublished Master of Sacred Theology thesis, Biblical Seminary in New York, 1946. FMHC

OUR FREE METHODIST Missions in Africa to April, 1907. Mrs. Chloe Anna Broadhead (Sanford), ed. Pittsburgh, Pennsylvania: The Aldine Print Co., 1908. 77pp. FMHC RWC SPU

REED, Nellie A. Ntombinkulu (Big Girl), or A Zulu Girl in Fair View Girls' School, Natal, South Africa. Chicago, Illinois: Free Methodist Publishing House, 1914. FMHC

REED, Nellie A. World Treasure Trails: Africa. Winona Lake, Indiana: Woman's Missionary Society, c1936. 127pp. FMHC RWC

ROOT, Helen Isabel. Our Africa Work: A Brief History of the Free Methodist Mission in Africa. Chicago, Illinois: Woman's Missionary Society, 1928. 45pp. FMHC RWC

SMITH, C. Stanley. Road to Revival - The Story of the Ruanda Mission. London, England: Church Missionary Society, 1948. FMHC (Refers to FM mission)

SMITH, Rose H. Youth's Incense or Life and Writings of Blanche Charlotte Smith. A Young African Saint. Cincinnati, Ohio: God's Bible School and Revivalist, n. d. FMHC

THEN Jesus Came. True Stories of Africa Children. Winona Lake, Indiana: Woman's Missionary Society, 1959. FMHC

WILLIAMSON, Glen. Frank and Hazel: The Adamson's of
Kibogora. Winona Lake, Indiana: Light and Life Press,
1972. FMHC

Missionary family to Kibogora, Africa.

CHINA, TAIWAN, and HONG KONG

APPLETON, Mrs. Pioneer Free Methodist Work in China.
Unpublished manuscript. No. 80, Documentary Record.
Free Methodist Historical Center.

FREE METHODIST Church. Entering the Open Door in Formosa.
James Hudson Taylor, ed. Winona Lake, Indiana: Light
and Life Press, 1956. 96pp. FMHC

HOGUE, Emma. China: A Mission Study for Juniors. 2nd
ed. Winona Lake, Indiana: Light and Life Press, 1920.
FMHC

HASLAM, Robert, et. al. Miracle in Mindanao and Other
Stories of Hong Kong, Taiwan and the Philippines.
Winona Lake, Indiana: Light and Life Press, 1974. FMHC

CYC/JMS Series.

ROOT, Helen Isabel. A Corn of Wheat, the Life Story of
Clara Leffingwell. Winona Lake, Indiana: Woman's Missionary Society of the Free Methodist Church, 1943.
105pp. FMHC RWC SPU

SAYRE, Mary Geneva. Missionary Triumphs in Occupied China.
Winona Lake, Indiana: Women's Missionary Society of
the Free Methodist Church, c1945. 207pp. FMHC RWC
SAC

SAYRE, Mary Geneva. On the Brink. Written with Glen Williamson. Winona Lake, Indiana: Free Methodist Publishing House, 1974. 103pp. FMHC

China in the midst of the Communist take-over.

SCHERER, Frances. George and Mary Schlosser: Ambassadors
for Christ in China. Winona Lake, Indiana: By author.
1976. FMHC

SELLEW, Walter. Clara Leffingwell. Chicago, Illinois:
Free Methodist Publishing House, c1907. 320pp. FMHC
RWC

TSUCHIYAMA, Tetsuji. Victory of the Cross. n.p., 1945.

WILLIAMSON, Glen. Geneva. Winona Lake, Indiana: Light
and Life Press, 1974. FMHC

The story of Geneva Sayre's missionary labor in China.

WINSLOW, Carolyn V. China's Four Sons. Winona Lake, Indiana: Light and Life Press, 1965. FMHC

Story of four men, sons of Free Methodist missionaries,
who became Free Methodist missionaries themselves.

WINSLOW, Carolyn V. Tomorrow. Winona Lake, Indiana:
Young People's Missionary Society, 1945. FMHC RWC

Story of Free Methodist mission in China.

DOMINICAN REPUBLIC and HAITI

GILMORE, Alene. Treasure in the Dominican. Winona Lake,
Indiana: Light and Life Press, 1964. FMHC

JOHNSON, Pearl Vennard. Our Neighbors, the Dominicans.
Winona Lake, Indiana: Woman's Missionary Society of
the Free Methodist Church. 1942. 142pp. FMHC RWC

NORBECK, Mildred E. The Challenge of the Hills. Apollo,
   Pennsylvania: West Publishing Co., 1947. 223pp.
   FMHC   SAC

On Haiti.

NORBECK, Mildred E. The Haitian Challenge and You! In-
   tercession City, Florida: Great Commission Crusades,
   1965. 166pp. FMHC   SAC

EGYPT

EGYPT Free Methodist Church. Original Minutes of the
   Egypt Church beginning with the 9th session, 1917-1925.
   No. 55, Documentary Record. Free Methodist Historical
   Center.

WARNER, David S. Glimpses of Palestine and Egypt. Chicago, Illinois: W. B. Rose, 1914. 229pp. FMHC   SAC

INDIA

CASBERG, Jessie L. Dhatu and His Friends. Winona Lake,
   Indiana: Light and Life Press, n.d.   FMHC

CHALLENGE in Central India. Rolland N. Davis, ed. Winona
   Lake, Indiana: Light and Life Press, c1954. 278pp.
   FMHC RWC

Written by members of the Free Methodist Mission and Church
   in Yeotmal, M.P. India.

CLARKE, Ethel H. Mary E. Chynoweth: Missionary to India.
   Chicago, Illinois: Woman's Foreign Missionary Society
   of the Free Methodist Church, 1915. 166pp. FMHC
   RWC

DAVIS, Rolland N. Redeemed. A Remarkable Conversion in

72

Heart of India. The Story of Moses David, Superinten-
dent of the Eastern District, and Evangelist, India
Free Methodist Church. Wun, M.P. India. Winona Lake,
Indiana: Woman's Missionary Society, 1954. FMHC

FREE METHODIST Church. Booklet about Free Methodist Missionaries in India, n.p., 1931. RWC

HOGUE, Emma L. India: A Mission Study for Juniors. 5th
ed. Chicago, Illinois: Woman's Missionary Society,
1920. 57pp. FMHC

MCMURRY, V. G. Pioneer Free Methodist Work in India. Unpublished manuscript. No. 79, Documentary Record. Free
Methodist Historical Center.

ROOT, Helen Isabel. An Alabaster Box. The Life Story of
Grace E. Barnes. Chicago, Illinois: Woman's Missionary Society, 1929. 102pp. FMHC RWC

ROOT, Loretta P. and Ann Zahniser. Friends from the East.
Winona Lake, Indiana: Light and Life Press, 1971. FMHC

CYC/JMS series on India and Egypt.

ROOT, Loretta P. Patches. Winona Lake, Indiana: Light
and Life Press, 1938. FMHC

SOUTHWORTH, Effie. Letters from Effie Southworth from
India and "India Letter Links." Unpublished manuscript.
No. 4, Accession List. Free Methodist Historical Center.

TAPPER, Ruth M. The Full Years: The Life Story of Helen
I. Root. Winona Lake, Indiana: The Young People's
Missionary Society, c1948. 96pp. FMHC RWC

WARD, Ernest F. Echoes from Bharatkhand. Chicago, Illinois: Free Methodist Publishing House, c1908, 1913.

176pp.   FMHC   RWC

Includes chapters by Mrs. Phebe E. Ward.

WARD, Ethel Ellen. World Treasure Trails II: India.
    Winona Lake, Indiana: Woman's Missionary Society,
    1938.   FMHC   SAC

WARD, Ethel E. Mother of Moses. Poona, India: R. F.
    Couture, 1963.

WARD, Ethel Ellen. Ordered Steps; or the Wards of India.
    Winona Lake, Indiana: Light and Life Press, 1951.
    187pp.   FMHC   SAC   SPU

WARD, Phebe. Phebe Ward's Diary, 1896-1897. Unpublished
    manuscript. No. 52, Accession List. Free Methodist
    Historical Center.

Free Methodist Missionary to India.

JAPAN

DeSHAZER, Jacob. I was a Prisoner of Japan, n.p., 1949.
    FMHC

FENSOME, Alice. The Living Faith in Japan. Winona Lake,
    Indiana: Woman's Missionary Society of the Free Meth-
    odist Church, 1957.   FMHC   RWC

History of Free Methodist work in Japan.

GRAIN of Wheat, A: Memories of a Missionary, Eva Bryan
    Millikan. Tadashi Haga, ed. Free Methodist Koganei
    Church, n.d.   FMHC

HOGUE, Emma L. Japan: A Mission Study for Juniors. 3rd
    ed. Chicago, Illinois: Woman's Foreign Missionary

Society of the Free Methodist Church, 1920. 63pp. FMHC

KANEDA, Kazuo. Overshadowed Journey. Tokyo, Japan: Hope
    Press, 1963. 159pp. FMHC

Autobiography.

KLEIN, Mattias. By Nippon's Lotus Ponds: Pen Pictures of
    Real Japan. New York, New York: Revell, 1914. 228pp.
    FMHC

MYLANDER, Ruth. Japan Investment. Winona Lake, Indiana:
    Light and Life Press, 1944. FMHC   RWC

ODA, Bishop. Footprints. Life of Bishop Oda. n.p., n.d.
    FMHC

Written in Japanese. Tribute by Bishop Marston, p. 261,
on Free Methodist Bishop.

SNIDER, Lois. Snow Pearl: A Girl of Japan. Winona Lake,
    Indiana: Light and Life Press, 1968. FMHC

TSUCHIYAMA, Tetsuji. From Darkness to Light. Chicago,
    Illinois: Light and Life Press, 1927. FMHC

WATSON, C. Hoyt. DeShazer. Winona Lake, Indiana: Light
    and Life Press, c1950. 181pp. FMHC   RWC   SAC

DeShazer was converted while a Japanese prisoner of war
and became one of Japan's best-loved missionaries.

WILLIAMSON, Glen. Brother Kawabe. Winona Lake, Indiana:
    Light and Life Press, 1977. FMHC

MEXICO and PANAMA

BEEGLE, Burton Linton. Panama and the Canal Zone. Chicago,

Illinois: Woman's Missionary Society, 1920. 42pp.
FMHC   SPU

PEARSON, Benjamin Harold. Mexican Missions. Chicago, Illinois: Woman's Missionary Society of the Free Methodist
   Church, 1925.   63pp.   FMHC   SPU

PEARSON, Benjamin Harold. Off to Panama! A True Adventure Story of the Opening Doors for Christian Missions
   in Panama. Los Angeles, California: Harry Harper,
   c1935. 126pp.   FMHC   RWC · SPU

PEARSON, Benjamin Harold. Wings to Aztec Land. Winona
   Lake, Indiana: Light and Life Press, 1936.   FMHC

WILLIAMSON, Glen. Gonzalo of Mexican Missions. Winona
   Lake, Indiana: Light and Life.Press, 1976.   FMHC

Life story of Gonzalo Cisneros which includes the history
of the Free Methodist Mexican Mission.

NORTH AMERICA

BURNETT, Clyde J. Free Methodist Work Among Japanese in
   America. Winona Lake, Indiana: Woman's Missionary Society, n.d. 10pp.   FMHC

BURNETT, Lillian Pool. The Advent of Joy. Los Angeles,
   California: Los Angeles Free Methodist Church, 1965.
   FMHC

Mrs. Burnett tells of her work with Pacific Coast Japanese.
Printed in Japanese.

FIFTIETH Anniversary of the Los Angeles Free Methodist
   Church, 1919-1969. Frank Omi, ed. Los Angeles, California: Los Angeles Free Methodist Church, 1970.   FMHC

Written in English and Japanese.

FORTIETH Anniversary of Berkeley Free Methodist Church, 1916-1956. John Miyabe, ed. n.p., n.d. FMHC

Written in English and Japanese.

NORBECK, Mildred E. The Lure of the Hills. A Tale of Life in the Mountains of Kentucky. Revivalist Press, 1931. FMHC

SWEIGARD, Jean, et. al. Blackie Buffalo and Other Stories of North American Missions. Winona Lake, Indiana: Light and Life Press, 1967. FMHC

YAMADA, Mujako. Pacific Coast Japanese Conference of the Free Methodist Church. Unpublished Master of Religious Education thesis, Fuller Theological Seminary, 1966. FMHC

PHILIPPINES

LIGHTING the Philippine Frontier. Presented by Free Methodist Missionaries in the Philippines. Ruby Schlosser and Gertrude H. Groesbeck, ed. Winona Lake, Indiana: Woman's Missionary Society, 1957. 96pp. FMHC RWC

SCHLOSSER, John H. Church Planting in Mindanao. Winona Lake, Indiana: General Missionary Board, c1965. FMHC RWC

On a Free Methodist mission in the Philippines.

SCHLOSSER, John H. The Free Methodist Church in the Philippines: Our Heritage and History. Unpublished Master of Theology in Missiology thesis, Fuller Theological Seminary, 1977. FMHC

SOUTH AMERICA

MANNOIA, Florence and Lucy Huston. Amigos. Winona Lake,

Indiana: Light and Life Press, c1970. 64pp. FMHC
RWC

On Free Methodist Missions in Brazil and Paraguay.

CYC/JMS Series.

PEARSON, Benjamin Harold. The Monk Who Lived Again: A
Tale of South America. Winona Lake, Indiana: Light
and Life Press, c1940. 185pp. RWC FMHC

PEARSON, Benjamin Harold. Next! Our Sunday School Quest
in South America. Winona Lake, Indiana: Light and
Life Press, 1940. 94pp. FMHC RWC SPU

Free Methodist Missions in South America.

THOMPSON, William Ralph. Factors in the Establishing of
a Free Methodist Training School in Paraguay. S.T.B.
thesis, The Biblical Seminary in New York, 1950.

MISSIONS - General Handbooks and Encyclopedias
(No locations given)

DIRECTORY OF North American Protestant Foreign Missionary
Agencies. New York: Missionary Research Library, n.d.

ENCYCLOPEDIA of Missions, Descriptive, Historical, Bio-
graphical, Statistical. Henry Otis Dwight and H. Allen
Tupper, ed's. 2nd ed. New York, New York: Funk and
Wagnall Co., 1910.

FM - p. 241.

ENCYCLOPEDIA of Modern Christian Missions: the Agencies.
Burton L. Goddard, ed. Camden, New Jersey: T. Nelson,
1967. 743pp.

INTERPRETATIVE Statistical Survey of the World Mission of

the Christian Church. Summary and Detailed Statistics of Churches to Missionary Societies, Interpretative International Missionary Council, 1938.

MISSION Handbook. North American Protestant Ministries Overseas. Edward R. Dayton, ed. 10th ed. Monrovia, California: Missions Advanced Research and Communications Center, 1973.

FM - p. 232. Statistical report on missions, fields of service, number of personnel, and institutions fully supported by denominations.

NORTH American Protestant Ministries Overseas. 9th ed. Monrovia, California: Missions Advanced Research and Communication, 1970.

FM - pp. 80, 176, 188, 199. Statistical summary of missions listed by primary task, e.g., education.

WORLD MISSIONARY ATLAS. Harlan B. Beech and Charles H. Fahs, ed's. New York, New York: Institute of Social and Religious Research, 1925.

FM - p. 236. Contains Directory of Missionary Societies, statistics of Protestant missions, maps of areas that have missions and descriptive notes on countries with mission stations.

MISSIONS - General History of Free Methodist Missions (General Biography)

BURRITT, Carrie. The Story of Fifty Years. Winona Lake, Indiana: Light and Life Press, 1935. 213pp. FMHC RWC SAC SPU

The story of Free Methodist missions in Portuguese East Africa, South Africa, India, Japan, China, Dominican Republic and missions in America.

DOANE, J. "Reports from Church Assemblies." Christianity

79

Today, (July 17, 1964), p. 33.   SPU

An international organization called the Free Methodist
World Fellowship and Constitutional Council is created.

FREE METHODIST Church. Commission on Missions. Annual
    report of Free Methodist World Missions. Winona Lake,
    Indiana: Light and Life Press, 1963.   FMHC   SPU

Information on Literature ministry, VISA, education and
medical missions in the Free Methodist Church.

FREE METHODIST Church Commission on Missions. Mission
    Manual. Winona Lake, Indiana: Free Methodist Church,
    1966. 65pp.   SPU

ⅹ FREE METHODIST Church. General Missionary Board. Pro-
    ceedings of the Annual Meetings. 1909- .   FMHC   RWC

FREELAND, Mariet Hardy. Missionary Martyrs. Mary Louisa
    Ranf. Missionary to India: and a Sketch of the Life
    of Mary E. Carpenter, Missionary to Africa. Chicago,
    Illinois: T. B. Arnold, c1892. 310pp. FMHC   RWC

Also included are sketches of the lives of Mary E. North,
Charles Sumner Kerwood, Arthur Young Lincoln, Polly Abby
Lincoln, Jennie Roland Torrence and Eunice Knapp, mission-
aries in Africa.

HANDBOOK of Free Methodist Missions. H. F. Johnson, comp.
    Winona Lake, Indiana: Light and Life Press, 1941.
    131pp.   FMHC   RWC   SAC

HOWLAND, Carl Leroy. Manual of Missions. New York, New
    York: Fleming H. Revell, 1913. 176pp.   FMHC   RWC
    SPU

Contains information on religions of mission lands, mission field work, etc.

JOHNSON, Harry F. Heroes of Other Lands. Winona Lake,

Indiana: Light and Life Press, 1939. 160pp. FMHC RWC

KIRKPATRICK, Charles D. "Perspective: A Glimpse of Mission Trends." Light and Life, (February 9, 1971), p. 7.
FMHC   RWC   SAC   SPU

KIRKPATRICK, Charles D. "Perspective: Missions Is People." Light and Life, (April 10, 1973), p. 14.   FMHC
RWC   SAC   SPU

LAMSON, Byron S. Lights in the World: Free Methodist Missions at Work. Winona Lake, Indiana: General Missionary Board, c1951. 220pp.   FMHC   RWC   SAC   SPU

LAMSON, Byron S. To Catch the Tide. Winona Lake, Indiana:
General Missionary Board (Free Methodist Church), c1963.
123pp.   FMHC   RWC   SAC   SPU

Story of Free Methodist World Fellowship.

LAMSON, Byron S. Venture! The Frontiers of Free Methodism. Winona Lake, Indiana: Light and Life Press, 1960.
FMHC   RWC   SPU

"NINETY YEARS of Free Methodist Missions," Light and Life,
(October 21, 1975), p. 14.   FMHC   RWC   SAC   SPU

Summary of Free Methodist mission accomplishments.

TAPPER, Ruth M. Glimpses of Victory. Chicago, Illinois:
Y.P.M.S. Council of the Free Methodist Church, 1931.
94pp.   FMHC   RWC   SPU

TAPPER, Ruth M. Life Stories of Foreign Missionaries of
the Free Methodist Church Supported by the Young People's Missionary Society, 1931-1935. Winona Lake, Indiana: Y.P.M.S. Council, 1935. 270pp.   FMHC RWC SAC

WINGET, Banjamin. Missions and Missionaries of the Free
Methodist Church. Chicago, Illinois: Free Methodist
Publishing House, 1911. 124pp.   FMHC RWC SAC SPU

PERIODICALS - Free Methodist Periodicals

CANADIAN FREE METHODIST HERALD. 1- , 1922- . Moose Jaw,
Saskatchewan; Trenton, Ontario; Stirling, Ontario. FMHC
RWC   SAC

Published under the auspices of the Jurisdictional Conference of the Free Methodist Church in Canada.

CHRISTIAN MINISTER. 1-10, 1949-1958. Winona Lake, Indiana.   FMHC   SAC

Quarterly. W. C. Mavis, editor, is of Asbury Seminary,
Wilmore, Kentucky. The Christian Minister is for those
primarily within the evangelical movement.

CURRENT. 1-5, No. 2, 1968-1972. Winona Lake, Indiana:
General Strategy Council.   FMHC   SPU

Published 9 times yearly. Replaced the Sunday School
Journal and added material from other departments.

EARNEST CHRISTIAN AND GOLDEN RULE. Devoted to the promo-
tion of experimental and practical piety. 1-97, 1860-
Dec. 1909. Buffalo, Rochester, Chicago. FMHC   RWC
SAC   SPU

B. T. Roberts was editor from 1860-1893.

FREE METHODIST Book Bulletin. 1-?, 1943-1948?.   FMHC

FREE METHODIST PASTOR. 1- , 1974- . General Council
for Church in Mission of Free Methodist Church of North
America.

Monthly for 10 months.

GENERAL CONFERENCE DAILY. Greenville, Illinois: S.K.J.
Chesbrough. 1-?, 1886-1969. Published as Winona '74
Daily in 1974.   FMHC   RWC   SPU

Each day of the general conference proceedings and the pastoral addresses are recorded - includes many other news items and pictures from the General Conferences.

INTERRACIAL NEWS. 1-?, Feb. 1950-1956. Greenville, Illinois. FMHC (Editor, Gilbert James)

Official publication of the Department of Inter-racial Evangelism of the Free Methodist Church which is now part of the Department of Evangelistic Outreach.

JUST BETWEEN US. 1-21, No. 4, 1944-1968. Winona Lake, Indiana: Light and Life Press. FMHC

Published irregularly. Contains information on in-house personnel, news items about printing.

THE LAYMAN. Voice of the Light and Life Men's Fellowship. 1-?, 1948-?, Winona Lake, Indiana.

Forerunner of Thrust.

LIGHT AND LIFE. 1- , 1868- . Chicago; New York; Winona Lake, Indiana: Jan. 1868-June, 1970 as Free Methodist. FMHC RWC SAC SPU

LIGHT AND LIFE HOUR TRANSMITTER. 1- , 1946- . Winona Lake, Indiana: Light and Life House, 1946? as Light and Life Hour. FMHC SPU

Monthly.

SUNDAY SCHOOL JOURNAL. 1-52, No. 12, 1916-1967. Winona Lake, Indiana: Sunday School Department of the Free Methodist Church. 1916-1953 as Sunday School Worker. FMHC RWC SAC

THRUST. 1- , 1959- . Winona Lake, Indiana: FMHC

Published irregularly but not less than quarterly. Paper
of the Light and Life Men. Forerunner was The Layman,
Voice of the Light and Life Men's Fellowship. Since March-
April, 1973, Thrust has been inserted in the Light and
Life magazine under its own name.

YOUTH IN ACTION. 1- , 1942- . Winona Lake, Indiana.
    1942-1954 as YMPS News. 1955-1956 as FMY News.   FMHC
    RWC   SAC   SPU

Monthly. Twelve issues per year to 1947 then scattered
and now 9 issues per year.

PERIODICALS - Missions

CONGO-NILE NOTES. From Ruanda-Urundi, Central Africa, on
    The Watershed of the Congo-Nile River Systems. 1924?-
    1946.   FMHC

Yearly.

ECOS EVANGELICOS. 1- , ?- . Dominican Republic.

Periodical printed in the Dominican Republic in Spanish.

ENCOUNTER. 1- , ?- . Winona Lake, Indiana: General
    Missionary Board.

Twice a year for missionary candidates and prospective
candidates.

INDIA LETTER LINKS. Your Missionary Friends Past and Pre-
    sent of the Free Methodist Church in India. 1-?, 1930-
    1958?. Poona, India: Oriental Watchman Publishing
    House.   FMHC   RWC

Yearly.

INHAMBANE TIDINGS. 1-?, 1911-1959. Inhambane, Mozambique.
   FMHC

Yearly.

MISSIONARY TIDINGS. 1- , 1897- . Chicago; Winona Lake,
   Indiana: Woman's Missionary Society of the Free Methodist Church.   FMHC   RWC   SAC   SPU

Monthly. Contains articles and pictures on Free Methodist
Churches and missions in 24 countries. It also is the pro-
motional magazine of the WMS.

MISSIONS OUTLOOK LEADERSHIP LETTER. 1- , ?- . General
   Missionary Board.   FMHC

Quarterly. For pastors and missions education directors.

NEWS AND VIEWS. 1- , 1962- . Winona Lake, Indiana:
   Free Methodist World Fellowship.   FMHC

Yearly through 1971 then twice a year.

NZIRA IBONEYE. 1- , ?- . Kibogora, Rwandu, Africa.

SHORTWAVE. 1- , ?- . Winona Lake, Indiana: General
   Missionary Board.

Five or six times per year.

PRAISE AND PRAYER. 1- , ?- . Kaifeng, China.

SCRIPTURE - GENERAL WORKS

DEMARAY, Donald E. Bible Study Source Book. Grand Rapids,
   Michigan: Zondervan, c1964, 1972.   FMHC

DEMARAY, Donald E. Bible Study Source Book. Grand Rapids,

Michigan: Zondervan, 1972.   FMHC

SHELHAMER, Elmer E.   Pointed Bible Readings on Various
    Subjects. Atlanta, Georgia, n.d. 160pp. FMHC   SAC

SIMS, Albert.   Helps to Bible Study with Practical Notes
    on the Books of Scripture. Designed for Ministers,
    local preachers, S. S. teachers, and all Christian
    Workers. Uxbridge, Ontario, 1886. 196pp.   FMHC

WARNER, David S.   The Book We Study: A Brief Tribute to
    the Holy Scriptures. Chicago, Illinois: W. B. Rose,
    1921.   FMHC

SERMONS

BAKER, Harold Edwin.   Sparks from the Anvil of Truth.
    East Liverpool, Ohio, 1944. 175pp. FMHC

BASTIAN, Donald N.   Along the Way. Winona Lake, Indiana:
    Light and Life, 1977.   FMHC

Sermons on contemporary topics.

BEAMS Of Light on Scripture Texts. A. Sims, comp. Tor-
    onto, Ontario, Canada: By compiler, n.d.   FMHC

BOYD, Myron F.   Flame of a Century: What Made It Burn?
    Radio Messages on John Wesley and Early Methodism.
    Winona Lake, Indiana: World-Wide Gospel Broadcast,
    1958.   FMHC   RWC

Myron F. Boyd delivered his messages on the "Gospel Clinic"
    and the "Light and Life Hour."

BOYD, Myron F.   To Tell the World: Thirty Radio Messages.
    Winona Lake, Indiana: Light and Life Hour, c1964.
    196pp.   FMHC   RWC   SAC

CROCKETT, H. L. Sermons of Rev. H. L. Crockett. Unpublished manuscript. No. 37, Documentary Record. Free Methodist Historical Center.

DEMARAY, Donald E. Loyalty to Christ. Sermons with Prayers for the Easter Season. Grand Rapids, Michigan: Baker Book House, 1958. FMHC RWC

FAIRBAIRN, Charles V. Tarry Ye and Other Sermons and Studies. Winona Lake, Indiana: Light and Life, 1943. 131pp. FMHC

FAIRBAIRN, Charles V. Tarry Ye and Other Sermons and Studies. 2nd ed. Winona Lake, Indiana: Light and Life Press, 1948. 131pp. RWC SAC FMHC

GRIFFITH, George W. Lest We Forget: Selected Messages for such a Day and Hour as This. Los Angeles, California: By compiler, 1939. 128pp. FMHC RWC

HOGUE, Wilson T. Retrospect and Prospect: A Semi-Centennial Sermon Preached by Bishop Wilson T. Hogue before the General Conference of the Free Methodist Church in Chicago, Illinois. Chicago, Illinois: Free Methodist Publishing House, 1911. FMHC

HOGUE, Wilson Thomas. Sermon Notes of Wilson T. Hogue. Unpublished manuscript. No. 16, Accession List. Free Methodist Historical Center.

HOGUE, Wilson Thomas. A Sermon, Preached at the Fiftieth Anniversary of the Marriage of Rev. Samuel K. J. and Ann E. Chesbrough. Together with the Experience of Ann E. Chesbrough. Chicago, Illinois: Free Methodist Publishing House, 1906. 64pp. RWC FMHC

HOGUE, Wilson Thomas. Contents of trunk belonging to Bishop Hogue. No. 57, Accession List. Free Methodist Historical Center.

Includes sermon notes, correspondence and journals.

SELLEW, Walter A. Semi-Centennial Sermon Delivered on the
Campground at Battle Creek, Michigan, July 3, 1910,
upon the occasion of the celebration of the Fiftieth
Anniversary of the Organization of the Free Methodist
Church. Chicago, Illinois: Free Methodist Publishing
House, 1910. FMHC

SELLEW, Walter A. Sermon Records (Journal), 1873-1928.
Unpublished manuscript. No. 78, Documentary Records.
Free Methodist Historical Center.

SHELHAMER, Elmer Ellsworth. Plain Preaching for Practical
People. Cincinnati, Ohio: God's Bible School and Revivalist, 1929. 288pp. FMHC RWC SAC

SHELHAMER, Elmer Ellsworth. Seven Searching Sermons. Cincinnati, Ohio: God's Revivalist, n.d. 64pp. SAC

SHELHAMER, Everett Edward. Heart Searching Sermons and
Sayings. n.p., n.d. RWC

SHELHAMER, Everett Edward. Pointed Preaching for Practical People. 2nd ed. Cincinnati, Ohio: God's Bible
School, 1932. 224pp. FMHC RWC

VINCENT, Burton Jones. As Ye Go, Preach: Outlines and
Notes from the Papers of Bishop Burton Jones Vincent.
Lena Duell Vincent, comp. Ann Arbor, Michigan: Cush-
ing-Malloy, 1975. 388pp. FMHC SAC

Burton J. Vincent was the 13th Free Methodist Bishop.

WHEATLAKE, S. K. Sermon Notes. Unpublished manuscript.
No. 18, Documentary Record. Free Methodist Historical
Center.

WHEATLAKE, S. K. The Touch of Fire: Sermons on Holiness.

Chicago, Illinois: Free Methodist Publishing House,
n.d. 125pp. FMHC RWC

WHITCOMB, A. L. Emmanuel and Stepping Stones to Union
with God. Winona Lake, Indiana: Light and Life Press,
n.d. 93pp. FMHC RWC SAC

SUNDAY SCHOOL CURRICULUM

ALDERSGATE Biblical Series. Donald M. Joy, ed. Winona
Lake, Indiana: Light and Life Press, 1960-   .

Book by book study of the entire Bible for use as elec-
tives in adult Sunday School classes. Includes Leader's
Guide, Study Guide, Daily Altar Guide. Aldersgate Association is made up of representatives of seven holiness
denominations who publish Aldersgate Sunday School Curriculum cooperatively.

ALDERSGATE Dialogue Series. Winona Lake, Indiana: Light
and Life Press. 197?-   .

Includes undated topical studies for use in the Sunday
School as elective courses for adults.

CHRISTIAN and Social Problems. Wesley Tracy, ed.
Kansas City, Missouri: Beacon Hill Press.

DARE TO Discipline. Wesley Tracy, ed. Kansas City,
Missouri: Beacon Hill Press.

DEVELOPING Christian Personality. Wesley Tracy, ed.
Kansas City, Missouri: Beacon Hill Press.

DISCOVER Your Bible. Wesley Tracy, ed. Kansas City,
Missouri: Beacon Hill Press.

HOLINESS -- Alive and Well. Wesley Tracy, ed. Kansas City, Missouri: Beacon Hill Press.

LOVE, Marriage-- and Other Hazards. Wesley Tracy, ed.
Kansas City, Missouri: Beacon Hill Press.

NOW Look of Evangelism. Wesley Tracy and Neil Wiseman, ed's. Kansas City, Missouri: Beacon Hill Press.

PRAYER That Really Works. Wesley Tracy, ed. Kansas City, Missouri: Beacon Hill Press.

SHAPE of Things to Come. Richard Lint, ed. Marion, Indiana: Wesley Press.

SINGLE in a Couples' World. Wesley Tracy, ed. Kansas City, Missouri: Beacon Hill Press.

STRATEGIES for Vital Christian Living. Wesley Tracy, ed. Kansas City, Missouri: Beacon Hill Press.

WHOLESOME Interpersonal Relationships. Neil Wiseman, ed. Kansas City, Missouri: Beacon Hill Press.

WHY Don't You Do Something, God? Wesley Tracy, ed. Kansas City, Missouri: Beacon Hill Press.

ALDERSGATE Doctrinal Studies. Winona Lake, Indiana: Light and Life Press, 196? - .

END TIMES - A Doctrinal Study on the Shape of Things to Come. Armor D. Peisker, ed. Marion, Indiana: Wesley Press, 1976.

ENTIRE Sanctification. Marion, Indiana: Wesley Press, 1964.

PEACE With God: Studies in Conversion. Marion, Indiana: Wesley Press, 1970.

ALDERSGATE Graded Curriculum. Winona Lake, Indiana: Light and Life Press, 19?? - .

ACTIVITY Time. 1- , Sept., 1969 - . Marion, Indiana: Wesley Press.

BIBLE Stories for Threes. 1- , 1961 - . Kansas City, Missouri: Beacon Hill Press.

BIBLE Stories for Twos. 1- , 1964 - . Kansas

City, Missouri: Beacon Hill Press.

EXPLORE. 1-6, No. 3, 1969-? . Winona Lake, Indiana:
Light and Life Press.

EXPLORER 1. 1- , 1975- . Winona Lake, Indiana:
Light and Life Press.

EXPLORER 2. 1- , 1975- . Winona Lake, Indiana:
Light and Life Press.

JUNIOR Teacher. 1- , 1969- . Winona Lake, Indiana:
Light and Life Press.

KINDERGARTEN Activities. 1- , 1969- . Kansas City,
Missouri: Beacon Hill Press.

KINDERGARTEN Bible Stories. 1- , 1969- . Kansas
City, Missouri: Beacon Hill Press.

KINDERGARTEN Teacher. ?- , ?- . Kansas City,
Missouri: Beacon Hill Press.

LEARN and Do. 1- , 1969- . Marion, Indiana: Wesley Press.

NURSERY Activities. 1- , 1969 - . Kansas City,
Missouri: Beacon Hill Press.

NURSERY Teacher. ?- , ?- . Kansas City, Missouri:
Beacon Hill Press.

PRIMARY Bible Stories. 1- , 1969- . Marion, Indiana: Wesley Press.

PRIMARY Friend. 1- , 1969- . Marion, Indiana:
Wesley Press.

PRIMARY Teacher. 1- , 1969- . Marion, Indiana:
Wesley Press.

PROBE Student. 1-3, No. 4, 1974-1977. Marion, Indiana: Wesley Press.

PROBE Teacher. 1-3, No. 4, 1974-1977. Marion, Indiana: Wesley Press.

QUEST Student. 1- , 1976- . Winona Lake, Indiana:
Light and Life Press.

QUEST Teacher. 1- , 1976- . Winona Lake, Indiana:
Light and Life Press.

SENIOR Teen Student. 1- , 1969- . Marion, Indiana:
Wesley Press.

SENIOR Teen Teacher. 1- , 1969- . Marion, Indiana:
Wesley Press.

TABLE Talk. 1- , 1969- . Winona Lake, Indiana:
Light and Life Press and Kansas City, Missouri:
Beacon Hill Press.

YOUNG Teen Student. 1- , 1969- . Winona Lake,
Indiana: Light and Life Press.

YOUNG Teen Teacher. 1- , 1969- . Winona Lake,
Indiana: Light and Life Press.

ALL-BIBLE Graded Series. Winona Lake, Indiana: Light and
Life Press, 197?-.

JUNIOR Manual. 1-3, No. 3, 1951-1953. Winona Lake,
Indiana: Light and Life Press.

TEACHING Beginners. 1-3, No. 3, 1951-1953. Winona
Lake, Indiana: Light and Life Press. Also published as Light and Life Beginner Teacher, 1951-
1952.

TEACHING Juniors. 1-3, No. 3, 1951-1953. Winona
Lake, Indiana: Light and Life Press. Also published as Light and Life Junior Teacher, 1951.

TEACHING Primaries. 1-3, No. 3, 1951-1952. Winona
Lake, Indiana: Light and Life Press. Also published as Light and Life Primary Teacher.

CHRISTIAN-LIFE Graded Bible Lessons. Winona Lake, Indiana:
Light and Life Press, 19??- .

LIGHT and Life Beginner Teacher. 1-4, No. 2, 1948-

1951. Winona Lake, Indiana: Light and Life Press.

LIGHT and Life Primary Teacher. 1-3, No. 2, 1949-
   1951. Winona Lake, Indiana: Light and Life Press.

INTERNATIONAL Uniform Series. Winona Lake, Indiana: Light
   and Life Press, 1885- .

   ARNOLD's Commentary. 1- , 1895- . Chicago, Illi-
      nois; Winona Lake, Indiana: Light and Life Press.
      Also published as Arnold's Practical Sabbath-
      School Lessons Commentary, 1895-1957.   FMHC   RWC
      SPU

   LIGHT and Life Adult. 1- , 1885- . Chicago, Illi-
      nois; Winona Lake, Indiana: Light and Life Press.
      Also published as Light and Life Scholar's Quar-
      terly, 1885-1921, and Light and Life Senior Quar-
      terly, 1921-1923.

   LIGHT and Life Junior Quarterly. 1-70, No. 4, 1891-
      1960. Chicago, Illinois; Winona Lake, Indiana:
      Light and Life Press.

   LIGHT and Life Junior Teacher. 1-4, No. 3, 1948-
      1951. Winona Lake, Indiana: Light and Life Press.

   LIGHT and Life Primary Quarterly. 1-70, No. 4, 1891-
      1960. Chicago, Illinois; Winona Lake, Indiana:
      Light and Life Press.

   LIGHT and Life Teachers' Quarterly. 1- , 1889- .
      Chicago, Illinois; Winona Lake, Indiana: Light and
      Life Press.

   LIGHT and Life Teachers' Quarterly for the Graded
      Primary Series. 1-9, No. 1, 1941-1949. Winona
      Lake, Indiana: Light and Life Press.

   LIGHT and Life Youth. 1-76, No. 3, 1885-1969. Chi-
      cago, Illinois; Winona Lake, Indiana: Light and
      Life Press. Also published as Light and Life
      Intermediate Quarterly, 1885-1924 and Light and
      Life Senior, Intermediate Quarterly, 1924-1951.

   LIGHT and Life Graded Series. Winona Lake, Indiana:
      Light and Life Press, 19??- .

JUNIOR Manual. 1-16, No. 4, 1953-1969. Winona Lake, Indiana: Light and Life Press.

KINDERGARTEN Activities. 1- , 1959- . Winona Lake, Indiana: Light and Life Press.

KINDERGARTEN Bible Stories. 1-16, No. 4, 1954-1969. Winona Lake, Indiana: Light and Life Press.

NURSERY Activities. 1- , 1959- . Winona Lake, Indiana: Light and Life Press.

NURSERY Bible Story Cards. 1-12, No. 3, 1958- ? . Winona Lake, Indiana: Light and Life Press.

PRIMARY Activities. 1-?, 1959-1969. Winona Lake, Indiana: Light and Life Press.

SENIOR Teen. 1-14, No. 1, 1956-1969. Winona Lake, Indiana: Light and Life Press. Also published as Senior Hi, 1956-1964.

TEACHING Juniors. 1-16, No. 4, 1953-1969. Winona Lake, Indiana: Light and Life Press.

TEACHING Preschool. 1-16, No. 4, 1951-1969. Winona Lake, Indiana: Light and Life Press. Also published as Teaching Beginners, 1951-1956.

TEACHING Primaries. 1-16, No. 4, 1953-1969. Winona Lake, Indiana: Light and Life Press.

TEACHING Senior Teens. 1-14, No. 1, 1956-1969. Winona Lake, Indiana: Light and Life Press. Also published as Teaching Senior Hi, 1956-1964.

TEACHING Young Teens. 1-16, No. 4, 1953-1969. Winona Lake, Indiana: Light and Life Press. Also published as Teaching Junior Hi, 1953-1964.

YOUNG TEEN. 1-16, No. 4, 1953-1969. Winona Lake, Indiana: Light and Life Press. Also published as Junior Hi Manual, 1953-1964.

STORY Papers. Winona Lake, Indiana: Light and Life Press, 19??- .

BIBLE Lesson Stories. 1-31, No. 4, 1930-1960. Providence, Rhode Island: Religious Press.

DISCOVERY. 1- , 1971- . Winona Lake, Indiana: Light and Life Press.

IN TOUCH. 1- , 1971- . Marion, Indiana: Wesley Press. Also published as Encounter, 1971-1976.

JUNIOR'S Friend. 1-14, No. 39, 1929-1942. Winona Lake, Indiana: Light and Life Press.

KINDERGARTEN Stories. 1-16, No. 4, 1954-1969. Winona Lake, Indiana: Light and Life Press.

LIGHT and Life Evangel. 1- , 1912- . Chicago, Illinois; Winona Lake, Indiana: Light and Life Press.

LILY of the Valley. 1-10, No. 12, 1897-1911. Chicago, Illinois: W. B. Rose.

OUR Young Folks. 1-10, No. 12, 1897-1911. Chicago, Illinois: W. B. Rose.

PRIMARY Bible Lesson Stories. 1-17, 1953-1969. Chicago, Illinois: Scripture Press.

PRIMARY Days. 17-19, No. 4, 1951-1953. Chicago, Illinois: Scripture Press.

PRIMARY World. 1-15, No. 3, 1955-1969. Winona Lake, Indiana: Light and Life Press.

ProTEEN. 1- , 1971- . Winona Lake, Indiana: Light and Life Press. Also published as Reachout, 1971-1976.

ROSE of Sharon. 1-10, No. 12, 1897-1911. Chicago, Illinois: W. B. Rose.

STORY Hour. 1- , 1885- . Chicago, Illinois: Winona Lake, Indiana: Light and Life Press. Also published as Light and Life Infant Class, 1885-1903; and Light and Life Primary Paper, 1903-1950.

STORY Trails. 1-87, No. 8, 1943-1971. Winona Lake, Indiana: Light and Life Press. Also published as

The High Trail, 1943-1950.

TEEN Time. 1-29, No. 8, 1951?-1971. Winona Lake,
Indiana: Light and Life Press.

YOUTH'S Temperance Evangel. 1-10, No. 12, 1897-1911.
Chicago, Illinois: W. B. Rose.

WOMEN IN THE CHURCH

FEAR, Leona. "My Dream." Light and Life, (June 17, 1976),
p. 10. FMHC RWC SAC SPU

FINE, Robert M. "Can Rachel Stand in the Pulpit?" Light
and Life, (May 14, 1974), p. 5. FMHC RWC SAC SPU

GROESBECK, Marian. "Perspective: The Role of Women Con-
tinues to Change." Light and Life, (May 14, 1974),
p. 19. FMHC RWC SAC SPU

JOHN, Edward C. "Bishops' Column: A Tribute to Free
Methodist Women," Light and Life, (March 14, 1974),
p. 18. FMHC RWC SAC SPU

Edward C. John was the 20th Free Methodist Bishop.

RICE, Wilda Bryan. "The Minister's Wife." Light and Life,
(February 8, 1972), p. 7. FMHC RWC SAC SPU

ROBERTS, Benjamin Titus. Ordaining Women. Rochester, New
York: The "Earnest Christian" Publishing House, c1891.
160 pp. FMHC RWC SAC SPU

Roberts examines the legal condition of women internation-
ally and the Old and New Testament statements on the proper
sphere of women. He then gives examples of women apostles,
prophets and deaconesses and the capacity of women for
evangelizing and governing nations.

SELLEW, Walter A. Why Not? A Plea for the Ordination of
those Women whom God has called to Preach the Gospel.
North Chili, New York: "Earnest Christian" Publishing
House, 1894. FMHC RWC

"WINONA '74: Keyword Action!" Light and Life, (July 23,
1974), pp. 3-8. FMHC RWC SAC SPU

WORK WITH YOUTH

FREE METHODIST Church. It's Time You Knew...the Facts
about the Ministry and Operation of the Young People's
Missionary Society through the Free Methodist Church
Around the World. Issued as Official Handbook by the
General Y.P.M.S. Council. Winona Lake, Indiana: The
Young People's Missionary Society, 1952. 124pp. RWC
SPU FMHC

JOY, Donald Marvin. A Survey and Analysis of the Experiences, Attitudes and Problems of Senior High Youth of
the Free Methodist Church. Unpublished M.A. thesis,
Southern Methodist University, 1960. FMHC

MARSTON, Leslie Ray. Youth Speaks. Winona Lake, Indiana:
Light and Life Press, 1939. 206pp. FMHC RWC SAC

Studies primarily of Free Methodist youth.

RICE, Alice F. Junior Missionary Society Guide. Winona
Lake, Indiana: Woman's Missionary Society, 1975. FMHC

ROSE, Mary Loretta O. Junior Missionary Society Handbook
for Superintendents. Winona Lake, Indiana: Woman's
Missionary Society, 1966. FMHC

SIGSWORTH, John W. Careers for Christian Youth. Chicago,
Illinois: Moody Press, 1956. FMHC

SUNDAY Evenings with Jesus - for Young People's Meetings.

Winona Lake, Indiana: Light and Life Press, 1936–
1959. 9v. FMHC

TODD, Floyd and Pauline Todd. Camping for Christian Youth.
A Guide to Methods and Principles for Evangelical Camps.
New York, New York: Harper and Row, 1963. FMHC

TODD, Pauline H. Truth in Action – Unusual Object Lessons
and Stimulating Ideas for Teachers of Truth. Winona
Lake, Indiana: Light and Life Press, 1961. 107pp.
FMHC

YOUTH Wants to Know. C. Mervin Russell. Winona Lake,
Indiana: Christian Youth Supplies, c1959. RWC FMHC

APPENDIX I

BISHOPS OF THE FREE METHODIST CHURCH

General Superintendents: (later called bishops)

Benjamin Titus Roberts	1860 - 1893
Edward P. Hart	1874 - 1908
George W. Coleman	1886 - 1903

Bishops

B. R. Jones	1894 - 1919	
W. A. Sellew	1898 - 1929	
Wilson T. Hogue	1903 - 1919	(1893-94 -- completed B.T. Robert's term while president of Greenville College)
William Pearce	1908 - 1947	
J. S. MacGeary	1911 - 1915	(Missionary Bishop - only one term)
W. H. Clark	1919 - 1925	
David S. Warner	1919 - 1927	
Arthur D. Zahniser	1927 - 1935	
George W. Griffith	1927 - 1936	
Burton J. Vincent	1931 - 1931	(died in first year of service)
Robert H. Warren	1935 - 1938	
Leslie R. Marston	1935 - 1964	
M. D. Ormston	1936 - 1958	
Charles V. Fairbairn	1939 - 1961	
J. Paul Taylor	1947 - 1964	
Walter S. Kendall	1958 - 1969	
Edward C. John	1961 - 1974	
Myron F. Boyd	1964 - 1976	
Paul N. Ellis	1964 -	
W. Dale Cryderman	1969 -	
Donald N. Bastian	1974 -	(first bishop assigned to Canada)
Elmer E. Parsons	1974 -	
Clyde E. VanValin	1976 -	

APPENDIX II - Special Collections of Material on Free
            Methodism

FREE METHODIST HISTORICAL CENTER

The Free Methodist Historical Center brings together
at Headquarters books, pamphlets, documents, pictures,
theses, and other valuable records relating to the history
of the church, including the history of major Methodism
dating back to John Wesley.

The cataloged research library of 5000 volumes includes
the Heritage Collection of books by Free Methodist authors;
bound copies of church-related periodicals; organizational
material; biographies; histories; and sections on doctrine
and distinctives of the church such as entire sanctification.
Books on related religious movements are included. All of
B. T. Roberts' published works are displayed.

The Missions Collection consists of diaries, journals,
record books, pictures, publications from the field, memor-
abilia and artifacts from early days of F.M. missions. Voices
of Free Methodism (bishops, general officers, etc.) and impor-
tant historic events in the life of the church are preserved
on cassette tapes and filed in the Center. There are "open
box" files in which are kept Annual Conference histories,
issues of conference papers, biographical material on conference ministers, and other materials pertaining to the
conferences and their local churches.

The Wesley Collection includes major holdings in the
life and writings of John Wesley including first editions
and many books and pamphlets published during his lifetime.
Most Wesley biographies and titles on his theology and influence are available at the Center. A large collection of
Wesley, Methodist and Free Methodist hymnals is included.

The history of Methodism in England and America is
thoroughly covered with many volumes of biography, general
histories, encyclopedias and reference works. Our holdings
in Wesleyana, Methodistica and Free Methodism are listed in
the Methodist Union Catalog: pre-1976 Imprints, edited by
Kenneth E. Rowe of Drew University Library.

Mrs. Evelyn Mottweiler, Librarian
Free Methodist Historical Center
Free Methodist World Headquarters
Winona Lake, Indiana 46590
1-219-267-7656   100

APPENDIX II

ROBERTS WESLEYAN COLLEGE ARCHIVES AND
CHESBROUGH-ROBERTS HISTORICAL CENTER

The Roberts Wesleyan College Archives is a repository for materials relating to the history and development of Roberts Wesleyan College (formerly Chili Seminary, A. M. Chesbrough Seminary and Roberts Junior College) containing administrative records, college and faculty publications, records of organizations, photographs and a small audio-visual collection.

The historical collection includes genealogical material, manuscripts, photographs, diaries and ephemera relating to the life, works and family of Benjamin Titus Roberts, founder of Chili Seminary (Roberts Wesleyan College) and principal founder of the Free Methodist Church.

Denominational works include yearbooks, books of discipline and digests of Free Methodist Law, denomination periodical publications, works on Free Methodist history, policy and doctrine, biographies of denominational leaders, a special collection of song and hymn books, materials on missions and benevolent institutions, and theses and dissertations on higher education in the Free Methodist Church.

The Library collection also includes holdings in Methodist Episcopal and Methodist History, the life and writings of John Wesley and the American Holiness Association.

The Archives and Historical Center displays are open to qualified researchers from 8:00 a.m. to 5:00 p.m. daily.

Mrs. Louise Campbell, Archivist
Kenneth B. Keating Library
Roberts Wesleyan College
2301 Westside Drive
Rochester, New York 14624
1-716-594-9471

APPENDIX II

SEATTLE PACIFIC UNIVERSITY

The Archives collection of Weter Memorial Library consists mainly of material pertinent to the Free Methodist Church and Seattle Pacific University. The collection is arranged in four parts - the cataloged books, the uncataloged (arranged by author), an alphabetical file of written material, and a picture file. The cataloged books consist of books necessary to a collection of Free Methodism (e.g., The Yearbook of the Free Methodist Church, Benjamin Titus Roberts' Holiness Teachings), and books concerning the beginnings of the then Seattle Seminary (e.g., Beers' The Romance of a Consecrated Life, Seattle Pacific's Bulletin).

The uncataloged collection contains a selection of hymnals, periodicals such as "The Earnest Christian," "The Free Methodist," and "The Light and Life," and Seattle Pacific's "Alumni Magazine." The collection also includes unique small Bibles as well as large beautifully bound Bibles. Mementos, pictures, and scrapbooks of past events of Seattle Pacific are displayed in the Archives. The alphabetical file ranges from information about each building's plans and history, each president's goals and accomplishments, to events such as commencement and open house. The picture file stores many photos of groups in the early days of Seattle Pacific, activities such as graduation and homecoming, and pictures of alumni as Free Methodist missionaries.

Mrs. Betty Fine, Head of Technical Services
Seattle Pacific University Library
3307 - 3rd Ave., West
Seattle, Washington 98119
1-206-281-2228

www.ingramcontent.com/pod-product-compliance
Lightning Source LLC
Chambersburg PA
CBHW020508030426
42337CB00011B/278